Relationship
Facts, Trends, and Choices

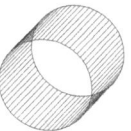

Author's Books
(As at 2016)

Non fiction

The Nature of Love and Relationships 2011, **2016** 2nd Edition
Doubts and Decisions for Living:
  Volume I: The Foundation of Human Thoughts   **2014**
  Volume II: The Sanctity of Human Spirit   **2014**
  Volume III: The Structure of Human Life   **2014**
Relationship Facts, Trends, and Choices   **2016**
The Mysteries of Life, Love, and Happiness   **2016**
Marriage and Divorce Hardships **2016**
Gender Qualities, Quirks, and Quarrels **2016**
Relationship Needs, Framework, and Models **2016**

Fiction

Persian Moons 2007, **2016** 2nd Edition
Midnight Gate-opener 2011, **2016** 2nd Edition
My Lousy Life Stories **2014**

Love and Relationships Series
The Bottom Line

Relationship
Facts,
Trends, and
Choices

Tom Omidi, Ph.D.

Copyright © 2016 by Tom Omidi

All rights reserved. No part of this book may be reproduced, translated, or transmitted in any form or by any means—graphic, electronic or mechanical, including photocopying, recording, taping or information storage or retrieval systems—without the prior written permission of the publisher or the author.

Library and Archives Canada Cataloguing in Publication

Omidi, Tom, 1945-
Relationship facts, trends, & choices : the bottom line / Tom Omidi.

(Love and relationships series ; 1)
ISBN 978-0-9938006-5-8 (paperback)

1. Man-woman relationships. 2. Interpersonal relations. 3. Love. 4. Interpersonal conflict. 5. Couples. 6. Couples Psychology. I. Title.

HQ801.O454 2016   306.7   C2016-902404-0

Published by Eros Books,
Vancouver, British Columbia
Canada

contact@erosbooks.net

Printed in the United States

Contents

	Page
Introduction: The Bottom Line	1
The Main Fact	2
The Main Trend	4
The Main Choice	5

PART I: The Facts

Chapter 1	Building Our Mentality	11
Chapter 2	Personal Needs	17
Chapter 3	Partners' Personality	29
Chapter 4	Love and Happiness	35
Appendix 4-A	Personal Needs (Motives) behind Love	55
Chapter 5	Hormones and Gender Differences	57
Chapter 6	Social Environment and Values	63
Chapter 7	Relationship Perceptions	79
Chapter 8	Relationship Needs	85

PART II: The Trends

Chapter 9	Fundamental Trends	97
Chapter 10	Social and Moral Trends	105
	Is Year 2115 a Good Target?	107
Chapter 11	Personality and Gender Trends	113

PART III: The Choices

Chapter 12	Relationship Solutions	147
Appendix 12-A	Personality Aspects' Properties	157
	Self-awareness for improving our relationship	160
Chapter 13	Relationship Guidelines	163
Appendix 13-A	GARP's Objectives	170
Chapter 14	Government Role and Legal System	177
	The Timetable to Make Radical changes	182

Epilogue	187
Being Good and Enlightened	188
Conclusion	191

Introduction
The Bottom Line

Over 900 facts, trends, and choices about relationships in this book demonstrate the difficulty of satisfying this simple human need in the new era. They show the main sources of relationship conflicts and the consequential, rising personal frustration and depression. With our bizarre perceptions and expectations from relationships, we have gotten ourselves trapped in an agonizing web of complex dilemmas. Before getting into all these details, however, the following main fact, trend, and choice reveal the bottom line:

The Main Fact
Our understanding of love and relationships
is wrong.

The Main Trend
Relationship conflicts have gotten out of hand
and the situation will continue to worsen.

The Main Choice
Only a drastic change in our mentality can save the
future of relationships.

Here, this is the shocking bottom line about love and relationships. Unless you truly sense and agree with this perspective, reading the rest of this book or following the prevalent shallow gimmicks to salvage your relationships would prove of little value. Of course, this book might at least help you think a bit deeper about love and relationships. Yet, at the end, you must believe in the above viewpoint wholeheartedly if you wish to live a more productive life with less stress from relationship paradox. Otherwise, looking for quick solutions or an ideal partner would continue to be futile. You would only heighten your inner conflicts and move from one relationship to the next in vain.

Therefore, ask yourself, now and after reading this book, whether you are sincerely convinced to change so many facets of your life gradually and painstakingly. You need patience and deep conviction to rebuild a constructive and manageable relationship atmosphere, or alternatively pursue a single life more resolutely as a creative, viable option. Unfortunately, most of us often fail in our relationship endeavours due to our naïve views and approaches toward this contentious social issue. We just keep feeding our misperceptions and then wonder why our relationship conflicts only get more enigmatic while our sense of loneliness heightens too.

The Main Fact

Almost everybody assumes to understand relationship facts and problems, as if s/he were a relationship guru intuitively. We trust our intuition too much. We believe that our imagination of relationships, based on our impressions from our whimsical surroundings and movies, are accurate and reliable. We are quite adamant and arrogant about our viewpoints and the kind of strategies that can make our relationships work perfectly. The only problem we see is our partner's lack of sound judgment, conscience, and compassion. Otherwise, our relationships would work fine! If only s/he stopped being so stubborn and selfish all our problems would be solved, we imagine. However, these assumptions, convictions, and impressions are absolutely false and misleading. The reason is that our knowledge of relationships is faulty and our analytical capacity regarding relationships is too limited. Our emotional tendencies, social pressures, and Ego always hinder our grasp of relevant factors important for the success of relationships.

Naturally, our goal is to bring compassion and peace to our relationships and lives. However, we end up causing ourselves more hassle when we do not understand the main purposes of relationships and instead focus on some untenable, selfish expectations. We do not know how to live independently, either, to be immune against the growing hassles of relationships. Thus, we pursue some shallow relationships and life purposes aimlessly while our painful search for a soul mate continues.

Sometime, we might even go one step further and courageously convince ourselves that time has come to change our own mentality—instead of our partner's—to save our relationship. However, at the end we fail, because we do not realize the full scope of efforts and sacrifices required for changing our mentality effectively. We neglect that building up a major commitment and enhancing our self-awareness demands enormous personal conviction and a gradual change of our lifestyle. The change of mentality is a difficult task because we must suddenly think outside the box, often against the confusing social values and norms.

Nevertheless, we must ultimately refine our understanding of relationships, individually and collectively, in a major way or endure lasting pains. Our present attitude toward relationships can in fact lead to the demise of humanity if most of us remain incapable of relating and helping one another. Only if enough people appreciate the need for change, we might be able to build a social system that supports a new vision of relationships. We may agree eventually that the emphasis must be put on teamwork and selflessness, instead of fake individualism, equality, and similar misleading criteria. We must define valid relationship purposes, according to some basic guidelines, and learn to respect the sanctity of relationships as an independent entity with unique needs of its own.

Several hundred facts explained in this book about relationships support the *main fact* stated above. These facts, with various degrees of urgencies, should convince us that our perceptions of relationships and pursuing them within the present framework would only frustrate us and make future generations' life even more difficult. The trends in recent decades clearly demonstrate these facts. Accordingly, our choices at so many levels are rather obvious, too, if only we stop and think a bit more practically. All the trends and choices discussed in this book are becoming facts of life rapidly, while the amount of depressing facts overwhelming our lives is increasing regularly. They all indicate that we must study our relationships more seriously and behave a bit more rationally. **Our present understanding of love and relationships is wrong.**

The Main Trend

Our relationships have been shaping around some showy and shallow social values that we have been embracing so keenly in recent decades. We have become addicted to materialism, judge one another based on superficial notions, and choose our partners according to wrong criteria and through erroneous mechanisms. Even when we are less calculating and depend on love to build a relationship, we are unaware of the more important factors that make a relationship successful. We are unaware of the specific relationship needs that we must satisfy before even thinking about our personal needs. Instead, we have allowed broad social trends, including greed, arrogance, disregard for environment, and corruption guide our expectations from relationships in recent decades as well.

As another prevailing trend, we look for quick fixes in all aspects of our lives without understanding the effect of our actions and decisions down the line or for future generations. We dismiss the fact that our obsession to focus on our immediate selfish needs sabotages our chance for building a lasting relationship. We have all along tried to deal only with the symptoms of relationship breakdowns instead of looking for the inherent problems of relationships nowadays. The trend is to trust our own guts and maybe some crooked social norms to set the standards for tolerance in relationships. We like to live 'in the now,' instead of creating some form of guidelines to help us relate more humanely more permanently for achieving the long-term advantages of being in a relationship.

Unfortunately, all the trends reveal that our relationships have become a victim of social issues deteriorating fast in all aspects of our lives and manifesting in the form of phony values and lifestyles. **Relationship conflicts have gotten out of hand and the situation will continue to worsen.**

The Main Choice

We must make many tough choices in life to stay sane and prosper as an independent person. Almost all those choices affect our views toward, and attitude in, relationships. Some specific choices directly relate to our relationships as will be discussed in this book. Yet, all our choices about various aspects of our lives affect everybody and our relationships in some manner. The reason is that our values and needs dictate our mentality and varied choices, including those related to our relationships issues and decisions.

Nevertheless, we must prepare ourselves to either live alone, at least mentally and emotionally, or learn some novel means of keeping a civilized relationship with a not-too-perfect partner. We might have a good partner, but when we do not understand each other and do not know how to relate, the sense of loneliness would feel even more excruciating than the option of living alone. Nevertheless, the outcome of our life choices is that we develop a particular mentality to spend our lives with someone or alone. Accordingly, the bottom line is that we should prepare ourselves to a life of semi-solitude supported by inner strengths and convictions whether we are in a relationship or not. However, for being in a relationship, we need more patience and a progressive mentality for relating to our partners practically and constructively. A major catastrophe in society is that almost no one is following either of these options effectively. They do not know how to relate in a relationship constructively, nor can they live as an independent person who enjoys his/her life of semi-solitude, satisfied with his/her own personal passions and thoughts. **Only a drastic change in our mentality can save the future of relationships.**

This book is divided into three parts: Facts, Trends, and Choices. The tiny numerals used for most paragraphs are to distinguish and emphasize the large number of relationship facts, trends, and choices, while maintaining the flow of discussions too. The numbering system is to encourage readers to pause and ponder every point at both personal and social levels, instead of reading the passages too fast. Every single one of these facts, trends, and choices deserve a deep scrutiny all by itself. Many of them deserve a long contemplation, maybe for a few days at least. That is the best way to raise our self-awareness and understand the intricacies of our relationships. Some of the points require an independent study and a book by themselves, in fact. They reveal a lot about the hurdles of building relationships and our tough task to make our lives more meaningful within or without a relationship.

Classifying and combining over thousand facts, trends, and choices, in an orderly manner, to create this concise book has been difficult. It is always easier to pick a handful of facts and write a book around them. For this book, however, a great deal of ideas have been grouped and presented in chapters while attempting to keep the flow of words and thoughts among the items grouped in each chapter. Yet, so much details and subsidiary facts have been left out to keep this book short. The main objective of this book is to emphasize on itemized facts, conclusions, and the bottom line for readers who prefer this type of outlined presentation. Readers interested in more details and technical analysis are encouraged to read *The Nature of Love and Relationships* by this author.

PART I

The Facts

Chapter One
Building Our Mentality

Some primary facts provide the foundation for building our mentality about relationships and thus they are listed in the first chapter. These facts are especially important for novice courting couples to consider diligently before getting into serious relationships.

1. More than 50% of marriages in modern societies lead to divorce and separation.
2. Furthermore, a large population has difficulty even starting a relationship due to the complexity of building a common ground for relating.
3. Even among the couples who remain married, a good majority consider their relationships unsatisfactory or torturous. They simply tolerate the situation because they are sceptical about the consequences of ending their marginal relationships.
4. Most of us deliberately ignore the above three fundamental facts when we fall in love and when we feel desperate for having a companion.
5. Naively, we prefer to dismiss the simple *fact* that so many marriage breakdowns represent something fundamentally

wrong with the way we perceive and handle marital relationships nowadays.
6. Due to various social deprivations, we actually feel too needy nowadays for a companion to both mitigate our loneliness and relieve our other sources of suffering. This growing neediness is much beyond our instinctual needs for mating and social belonging.
7. We have gradually come to view 'companionship' a basic need and not a medium range social need. Most of us consider it the highest prize God could bestow upon humans, not to mention the sexual benefits of relationships. This deep belief has evolved somewhat instinctually, but mostly through social conditioning in recent decades.
8. Combining the above seven facts, it becomes obvious that most people suffer due to relationships (whether they are in one or not), because they consider having a companion an essential need, which they remain unable to satisfy permanently, if at all.
9. Accordingly, another clear fact is that couples cannot *relate* effectively.
10. It also means that couples are not properly *trained* to maintain their relationships.
11. In fact, couples cannot even anticipate the basic hurdles of relationships or assess them realistically.
12. All couples, especially newlyweds, have wrong perceptions about the purposes and potentials of relationships. This ignorance is particularly harmful to them when they are either unconscious about the high chance of marriage breakdowns or prefer to ignore this alarming fact.
13. Furthermore, couples are not trained to work proactively from day one to protect their marriage from going stray on a wrong course. They are not even aware of the need for monitoring their relationships' health and the means of doing it.

14. Meanwhile, the old principles that kept marriages together are long gone and no new principles have been developed to keep couples alert in line with relationship needs in the new era.
15. With societies getting more complex every day, our lifestyles and convictions have changed drastically. Accordingly, our relationships have become quite difficult to understand and manage.
16. Our personal needs, insecurities, and idiosyncrasies have also been increasing rapidly in line with changes in social values. However, we not only do not appreciate the hazards of these rising personal flaws, but also justify our new needs and defects so obsessively and often arrogantly.
17. Yet, we notice our partner's simplest flaws quickly and nag about them impatiently.
18. We have difficulty accepting that people's personal defects are natural consequences of their genetic and upbringing conditions, all beyond their control.
19. Instead, we keep pushing our partners to change, or we retaliate to make them suffer.
20. At the same time, we are getting more obsessed every day about finding happiness and love in such a contaminated social environment.
21. We have become more demanding of our marriage partners, society, and ourselves.
22. Our unrelenting personal needs, especially individualism, is placing undue pressure on relationships and causing more frictions.
23. Conversely, personal stress from relationships is putting enormous pressure on society and the economy too.
24. In fact, social pressures make us needier for a companion, and in return, our failing relationships are ruining the foundation of social values and structure. This vicious cycle is running out of control. Thus, both society and individuals suffer deeper every day.

25. Social mechanisms and laws are not efficient anymore, either, to respond to the newer needs of relationships. Neither our religious guidelines, nor our legal systems can protect couples or offer them new ways of relating in a complex environment we have created for ourselves and cherish dearly.
26. We are ignoring the fact that family values are in need of major overhaul. We are ignoring the need for serious studies about relationships and their doomed destiny. Neither the public nor governments give enough priority to these fundamental social and personal issues.
27. Nobody actually seems to know how to go about finding solutions for our derailed relationships. Accordingly, people seem to have resigned to solely depend on the natural course of history to correct the rotting situation of relationships. However, this approach demonstrates only our wishful thinking that has no chance for success.
28. For a practical and lasting salvation of relationships, we need both personal and social efforts for: 1) an overhaul of couples' mindset, and 2) development of a set of guidelines to help them relate more effectively in their relationships. Why we cannot see this simple fact is ironic and amazing. Or maybe we know this, but do not have the expertise or motivation to do anything about it.
29. Obviously, we can never eliminate relationships conundrums fully due to humans' conflicting needs and instincts, hormones, Ego, and gender differences. However, we can make relationships smoother by following some basic guidelines, while we prepare ourselves more proactively for the inevitable hassles of relationships.
30. So far, we have ignored the need for radical solutions to make relationships more manageable in the new world.
31. We have failed to see that a new set of Generally Acceptable Relationship Principles (GARP) should be developed to match social changes in the new era.

32. We must propagate GARP actively in order to change couples' mentality about the nature of love and relationships and agree on the civilized means of relating. Maybe we can hope to get the full benefit of our efforts by the year 2115, if by then humanity still exists in a functional way. Yet, even gradual changes in social mentality can help us all in major ways immediately.
33. Creating a new atmosphere for relationships would not be easy and quick. People are not ready to give up their personal convictions and pleasures to improve their relationships. Yet, we must face this challenge eventually to save humanity and our souls from so much suffering in relationships.
34. Ultimately, our personal goal is to clarify the true nature of love and relationships, so that we may come to terms with ourselves personally for a more tranquil life in or out of a relationship. Once we learn to live without expecting love and relationships bringing us that elusive happiness, we might begin to enjoy our relationships too.

The bottom line is that:

A: We need to upgrade our mindset

35. Both our initial optimism about relationships (when we start one) and subsequent retaliations (when it fails) are destructive.
36. Our perspective of relationships is too naïve, unrealistic, and incompatible with the format of modern society. Overall, we must learn to lower our expectations from relationships in order to attend to our increasing personal needs independently.
37. We must prepare ourselves, both emotionally and financially, to deal with the high possibility of failure in our marriages and relationships.

38. We must admit that only by conscious efforts and major personal sacrifices a relationship might last on a long-term basis. Our present mindset (personal priorities) and social values make the job of prolonging our relationships extremely difficult, if not impossible altogether.

B. We must understand human limitations

39. The complexity of human cognition and behaviour, driven by a variety of personal needs, traits, and perceptions, causes all kinds of relationship problems.
40. The underlying causes of relationship failures remain beyond partners' control. In other words, partners cannot help the situation. They are helpless due to human's psychological defects and genetic built.
41. Our faultfinding attitude toward our partners is a futile exercise. In addition, our efforts to change others (our partners) are absurd, especially when the matter is pursued through retaliation and intimidation.

C. We urgently need new solutions and guidelines

42. Dynamic relationship principles are needed to reflect the realities of the modern world.
43. New guidelines are needed to facilitate individuals' drive to be independent, assertive, proactive, and make the best use of their lives.
44. Revolutionary social mechanisms and norms are needed to help us manage our relationships and possibly reduce their chances of failure.
45. Revolutionary laws must be devised to make separations easy and somewhat stress free.
46. Revolutionary social mechanisms and education are needed to prepare couples for the psychological effects of relationships, especially separation.

Chapter Two
Personal Needs

Our personal needs have risen exponentially in recent decades due to the pressures of consumerism and our urges to imitate others and the symbols of modernity. This huge increase in personal expectations has confused our senses about our natural needs and ruined our relationships too. The following facts reveal the nature of our personal needs, the problems they cause, and the ways we can mitigate their negative impacts on our relationships.

47. Humans are driven by a set of progressive needs. Basic needs, such as food and shelter, are at the bottom of this 'personal needs tree'. Our needs for social interaction and recognition stand in the middle. The higher needs consist of self-esteem and actualization. According to this theory, people climb up the 'needs tree' only as their lower needs are satisfied.
48. We usually have major difficulty satisfying our middle range needs, including relationships and recognition. Then we rarely find the opportunity to strive for our higher needs. Our obsession with our middle range needs hinders our chances to attend to the higher ones.

49. In particular, our struggle to find and keep a suitable companion proves too frustrating and time-consuming. Yet, despite our relentless efforts, this need (for a companion) remains substantially unfulfilled for most of us.
50. Accordingly, we lose our chances to spend enough time on our other personal or relationship needs. Especially, our needs for self-actualization, real individualism, and spirituality remain unfulfilled. Thus, we never learn to become a selfless and self-reliant person and enjoy the sense of contentment.
51. Meanwhile, we naively assume that relationships can magically fulfil our most prominent personal needs.
52. We also assume that relationships can somehow deal with all the idiosyncrasies that partners bring with them to this environment.
53. In reality, however, relationships only place more demands on partners.
54. Instead of satisfying our personal needs, relationships in fact cause more frustrations for couples by restricting their time, energy, and means of achieving their personal goals individually.
55. Couples ignore that often their own personal needs and expectations require adjusting—in order to improve their relationships—and not the attitude of their partners.
56. Our personal needs for more things and more compassion are merely raw obsessions that we have imposed upon ourselves by habit and imitation in modern societies.
57. Expecting relationships to serve our raw obsessions is even a more naïve and egotistical attitude.
58. Our personal needs are becoming too complex because the authentic and artificial ones are blending and creating new meanings and expectations beyond our apprehension and ability to satisfy. Yet, we must somehow learn to deal with all these needs.

59. We assume that our partners can (and must) respond to our rising personal needs, while we selfishly believe that those needs are sensible too.
60. We also imagine that our partners are psychologically equipped to respond to our particular needs (e.g. for compassion) at the exact time and manner we desire.
61. Overall, we assume that our partners are capable of making us happy. This is a common mistake that couples make when they start a relationship.
62. Therefore, contrary to our naïve presumptions, our personal needs usually get frustrated instead of fulfilled when we start a relationship.
63. In all, we must find ways of fulfilling our personal needs (e.g., finding happiness) independently so that the burden on relationships is reduced.
64. It is depressing to see that finding a suitable companion has become such a challenging and frustrating endeavour despite the increasing number of matchmaking services and meeting places.
65. Unfortunately, nobody knows the needs and demands of relationships nowadays and instead focus on their personal needs and demands.
66. Couples also fail because no realistic definition of 'relationship needs' exists to prepare them for the challenges of companionship in the new era amidst all other daily life demands. 'Relationship Needs' is explored in Chapter Eight.
67. Couples' lack of knowledge about the specific needs of relationships has caused them lose their sense of objectivity and thus many relationships get into trouble quickly nowadays.
68. Furthermore, the atmosphere for personal need fulfilment is not calm and logical nowadays. People get hysterical when their imaginary needs are not satisfied.

69. Increasingly, we witness people's hysteria for not succeeding to climb up the personal needs tree quickly enough and fulfil their ambitions, find happiness, or even find a reliable companion.
70. Thus, learning about the nature and authenticity of our personal needs, and motivations behind them—mainly through self-awareness—can help our relationships immensely.
71. In fact, the only way couples may build or save their relationships is to pursue a serious means of self-analysis, enhance their awareness about the complexity of human needs and behaviour in general, and learn how partners' idiosyncrasies infect their relationships.
72. Our personal needs are developed and triggered by a wide range of inner and outer forces. Outer forces refer to socioeconomic environment, up-bringing, etc. Inner forces comprise of:
    - Instincts
    - Genetics
    - Habits (conditioning)
    - Reactions (impulses)
73. Inner forces mainly constitute our inherent or absorbed characteristics. We hardly have any control over these traits.
74. Our goal for studying the inner forces is to increase self-awareness and thus stir objectivity into our relationships. Then, through self-awareness, couples learn that so much of their partners' personalities are also developed by forces beyond their control.
75. Our biggest misperception is that our partners are in control of their personalities. We forget that both inner and outer forces largely cripple people mentally to control their Ego and logic.
76. As a symbol of civilization, we have developed laws, ethics, and etiquettes because we believe that people's urges and actions are often fuelled by erratic forces mostly beyond their control. Yet, in our relationships, we keep forgetting or

ignoring the fact about humans' inability to be good or reliable.
77. We have little patience for imperfections because we arrogantly assume that we are perfect ourselves. Furthermore, we expect others to be perfect, too, according to our perceived definition of perfection, of course. These two misleading presumptions are actually the influence of our inner forces dictating our judgment and dulling our objectivity.
78. People assume that relationships can fulfil their personal needs, or empower them to do so personally. In reality, however, they find more restrictions in achieving them. Each partner gets frustrated because:
- Fulfilling even his/her basic needs, including sex, is suddenly at the mercy of someone else.
- The cost of satisfying his/her needs often seems to be too high and against his/her convictions, integrity, and sense of independence. The cost mostly entails some type of humiliation he/she must bear to accommodate his/her partner.
- He/she cannot seek relief anywhere else because of his/her commitment to their relationship. For example, if he/she seeks sex outside of their failing relationship, he/she faces the charge of adultery. It would be a taboo to satisfy a strong natural urge, a basic need that he/she could satisfy almost at will prior to entering a relationship.
- The situation spins out of control, because his/her partner's unending demands are unrealistic and it is not easy to abandon the relationship either. The relationship stays in a stalemate indefinitely.
79. We seek a companion to satisfy three major personal needs: Sex, compassion, and love. These needs are the three pillars of relationships.
80. In the present frustrating environment, partners' needs for sex and compassion are jeopardized and they face mental and physical hardship. Those who insist on finding 'love' in

a relationship, too, are in an even tougher position, because their expectation is beyond the limits of a normal relationship to begin with.

81. Yet, often, neither partner is at fault in these situations. They are both victims of their *complex needs* and irreversible idiosyncrasies. They have been conditioned in society to set high expectations for relationships. 'Complex needs' is meant here to reflect both our instinctual needs, such as sex, and those artificial ones, such as need for more things and more compassion. After all, these artificial needs are the symptoms of new lifestyles in modern society and we are helplessly obsessed by them.

82. Even partners' retaliations, when their complex needs are ignored, might be considered natural if we accept them as defence mechanisms. It will be discussed in the future chapters that partners' many personality flaws force them to react irrationally. To them, reacting or retaliating is their only tool to survive in this chaotic society. Their only guilt is that they have naively believed that they would get their needs satisfied faster in a relationship. They have naively ignored the fact that their partners are entering relationships with many urgent needs and demands of their own.

83. In addition, couples naively believe that they can convince their partners better through retaliation and by playing games. Most often, actually, retaliation and playing games are all they know for controlling their relationships and partners.

84. Most relationships would have been considered acceptable if couples were not misled by their superficial needs. For example, partners believe that they deserve high attention from their companions and actually be 'spoiled' by them rather regularly. Or as they get old, they only see the aging of their partner and not their own. Therefore, they try to revive their youthful memories with another person who is

not so old and cranky like their spouses, and flatters them too.

85. That is, people's seeming urgent needs make them lose sight of their longer-term needs that are often in conflict with the first group, e.g., their needs for more sexuality and youthful experiences.

86. One particular inner conflict stays with us for the rest of our lives. It arises when our two fundamental needs for dependence and independence keep competing and clashing constantly in our mind.

87. In fact, all our needs are often at the mercy of our needs for dependence and independence. Our other needs (even our basic need for food) are boosted or dampened by our prominent need for independence (or dependence) regardless of the consequences.

88. As we proceed through life, the number of our dependencies keeps rising, while we keep struggling to develop our unique identity and independence. We get frustrated often when our independence is tainted by our need for dependence on other people and society.

89. We hate the way our partner is squashing our independence. However, we also hate that we cannot depend on them enough. The level of conflict between our needs for dependence and independence keeps rising and putting pressure on relationships.

90. Especially, with the added emphasis on individualism and independence in modern societies, personal conflicts due to the inner needs for both dependence and independence have become too prominent and more widespread in society.

91. Creating and maintaining a balance between our conflicting needs for both independence and dependence is a tough job, even if we assume such a balance can be found.

92. In general, independence requires (and leads to) a lot of isolation and self-reliance. On the other hand, dependence is mostly synonymous with (need for) compassion.

93. Our partners and society in general do not know how to cope with our need for dependence. Often, they actually ridicule and take advantage of our perceived weakness, i.e. our inability to be independent.
94. Our inner conflicts actually heighten when we try to pretend to be more independent than we really feel we are, or can handle.
95. By exaggerating our need for independence, we are in effect imposing another set of artificial expectations on ourselves, which are unachievable.
96. At the same time, we are jeopardizing our chances to fulfil our need for dependence. We keep alienating our partners by our exaggerated show of independence. These superficial needs and situations cause more inner conflicts for each partner, as well as more clashes between partners.
97. People become aggressive in order to show assertiveness, mostly because they do not know the delicate art of assertiveness for fulfilling their needs.
98. The artificial need to *show off* our independence, as a symbol of freedom and identity, has in effect become counterproductive for both our individuality and relationships.
99. The bottom line is that partners' need for dependence is undervalued at so many levels by our modern lifestyles, values, and social pressures. It is trendier to show one's aptitude for individualism. Therefore, people pretend to be independent in order to fit and survive.
100. Obviously, the smart thing nowadays is to not depend on others or their words. They simply cannot deliver because of the limitations in their own lives and personality, and not necessarily out of malice.
101. Meanwhile, there is an ongoing struggle between partners to maintain a balance of power in order to stop each other from dominating their relationship.
102. Everybody likes more independence for themselves but less for their partners.

103. With freedom (and independence), most people are mainly thinking about freedom to explore sexuality and love. This is an automatic reaction to our philosophy about life being short and living only once.
104. Couples' struggle to cope with their needs for dependence and independence has led to a bizarre development: Some couples seek separation with the slightest inconvenience in their relationships; and some couples accept abuse and adultery because they are too apprehensive about loneliness and isolation. These prevalent extremes show the extent of value changes in new societies.
105. Overall, we are not as strong individuals as we often pretend to be in our exaggerated show of independence and individuality.
106. We are not equipped and strong enough to create a reasonable balance between our needs for dependence and independence in our relationships either.
107. The desire for wealth and power has ruined our capacity to grasp our very basic need for true independence, to free ourselves from people and symbols that constrict our ability to think straight and unselfishly. We pretend to be independent and free, but these gestures are usually too far from reality (our daily routines) and how we really feel.

The contentious issues about our personal needs for dependence and independence are summarized below in the remainder of this chapter:

108. We are not quite conscious of our conflicting needs for dependence and independence. Nor are we aware of the high repercussions of this conflict for us, our relationships, and society in general.
109. We do not know how to define or judge our personal needs for independence and dependence. We do not know how to be independent or dependent when we go about satisfying

these needs alternately on a regular basis. Some people pretend to be independent and needless when deep down their need for dependence is overwhelming. And some people damage their identity when they become submissive.

110. We play the kind of roles that society and people suggest, usually with the highest emphasis on independence, since we do not know how to set and keep a practical balance between our conflicting needs for independence and dependence. Yet, everybody has a different balance of needs for independence and dependence according to his/her personality. Ignoring one's particular needs (for dependence and independence) and sticking to some fake balance creates confusion and frustration.

111. Couples do not know how to discuss and match their needs for dependence and independence—mostly because it might require some kind of compromise, which would be against their presumed identity and independence. Therefore, they end up arguing about every detail or decision required for running their relationships.

112. Without knowing about our needs for independence and dependence and the balance most suitable for us, we expect our partners to behave as if they did know what the right balance should be. For example, we expect them to respect our independence when we suddenly feel it is time for us to be independent; we ask for a vaster boundary. Then, later, we expect them to be compassionate and caring as soon as we need their attention to satisfy our need for dependence.

113. We turn off our partners with our exaggerated show of independence and needlessness. And we confuse them with our silly roles and games to enforce our alternating needs for dependence and independence. These erratic interactions make partners' job to relate to each other difficult.

114. Meanwhile, power struggles to dominate our partners, and enforce our gender identities, postpone the matter of finding the right balance (between dependence and independence)

even further. Only arrogance and phoniness prevail in this kind of environment. All these conditions hinder the task of bringing objectivity and peace into relationships.

115. As social complexity and the public's intelligence increase every year, people's demands for both independence and dependence will rise.

116. They seek more independence because society pushes them to express themselves, and prove their identity, more explicitly. However, they also seek more dependence (need for a compassionate companion) because of the increased level of stress in their daily lives and the overall sense of loneliness. Therefore, instead of balancing their needs for dependence and independence, people struggle even more with their rising anxiety and inner conflicts.

117. The topics covered in this book demonstrate how the rising imbalance (between our needs for both independence and dependence) is forced upon us due to our lifestyles and mentalities.

118. Accordingly, relationships will become more instable in the future and their longevity will continue to decline.

119. Considering this inevitable prospect, it is crucial to ponder relationship facts, trends, and choices reiterated in this book very carefully, especially in terms of the 'radical changes,' suggested in Part III.

120. A side comment worth making, based on the above discussions, is that both our basic need for sex (including the urge for reproduction, especially for women) and our high-level need for selfless, spiritual love are instinctual needs. Therefore, it appears that we have created most of the medium-range personal needs through evolution and according to cultural conditions. As we have felt psychologically weaker and more vulnerable within new environments, we have developed all types of superficial needs to soothe our suffering and to deal with our dependencies on others. We have also introduced new social values and personal games to satisfy

our urgent need for a companion, but also as part of couples' power struggles, which would keeps rising in relationships.
121. The above facts provide further clues about the degrading state of relationships. They show that the faster our societies grow, the more superficial needs we impose on ourselves and our relationships, and the more complex the relationship environment gets.
122. As social values and personal needs of couples change during the course of history, the meaning, objectives, and format of their relationships change. Thus, they should be reassessed and redefined every few decades as well.

Chapter Three
Partners' Personalities

The effects of our vast superficial needs and the demand for social adaptation have made us phoney and we have lost our ability to feel and behave naturally. With our exaggerated identities and ideals, we do not know who we are.

123. The way we go about satisfying our personal needs portrays our 'personality.' Personality reveals i) our efforts to relate to the world, and ii) other people's perception of our efforts to relate to the world.
124. Studying human personality, and its impact on our lives, is highly urgent, because we are all striving to establish our identities individually and in relationships.
125. 'Personality' is an abstract concept, because it is only a reflection of who we want to be or try to be, not the true person we are. And, also, because personality remains largely a matter of judgment by others about who we are, again not the person that we really are. In all, 'personality' remains a complex dimension of human with very peculiar characteristics that are hard to pinpoint or predict, let alone manage.
126. At the same time, personality is the main tool and motivator to go about satisfying our personal needs. Accordingly, our

fake identities often confuse our minds and the course of our lives completely.

127. Personality also contains a large inventory of emotions and cognition. Thus, the shallow personalities that we try to adopt or imitate hurt us deeply too.

128. We love *who we believe we are* and thus avoid any advice or clues about the way our personality is hurting us or people around us. Accordingly, we seldom give ourselves a chance to find out *who we are*.

129. Unfortunately, we hate to agree that our new values and our personalities are too ambiguous (and shallow too), and they are becoming drastically detrimental to our happiness and health, as well as our relationships.

130. The distinction between good and bad is becoming too subjective nowadays. We depend on the authorities, celebrities, and propagandas to decide about good and bad. Our personalities evolve around the same values. Accordingly, defining and developing a balanced and useful personality have become too difficult.

131. The personality model presented here by this author, and in all his *relationships* books, has three components:

- **Ego** reflects (and drives) our desires, ambitions, sense of responsibility, defence mechanism, and all other traits that enable us to assert ourselves and protect our lives.
- **Self** contains our inner urges, love, integrity, inquisitiveness, potentialities, creativity and spirituality. This aspect of our personality reflects humans' soul and vulnerability.
- **Model** is the most practical aspect of our personality in the way it tries to help us adapt to social norms and get accepted and admired if possible. It is driven mainly by our conditional and adaptation needs.

132. Depending upon our genetics and experiences, each person's personality manifests by a different degree of Ego, Model, and Self.
133. The complexity of relationship interactions and communications is due to the way different personality aspects of partners react to one another in every situation without proper attention or intention.
134. Although we may apply any mix of the personality aspects in a special instance for a special purpose, we often adopt a fix personality profile that reflects a certain proportion of each aspect of personality.
135. Our actions and attitude reflect some degree of all three aspects of our unique personalities. However, we can witness how every one of our daily interactions has a tone in line with one particular aspect of our personality.
136. People often behave under the influence of a main personality aspect.
137. Our personality aspects create misperceptions when we are sending a message and also when we are receiving a message.
138. The irony is that we believe or pretend to be communicating with total honesty and integrity. We believe we are communicating with our Self. However, in reality almost all communications are contaminated by Ego and Model.
139. It helps our relationships, and life as a whole, if we learn to gauge and adjust the volume of these personality aspects regularly. We can make a habit of monitoring and distinguishing the personality aspects in our encounters and see which one is usually in control.
140. Keeping track of the interworking and manifestation of our personality aspects is the most important step toward self-awareness, which is obviously the best tool for improving our relationships. A useful process of self-awareness, and also minimizing relationship clashes, is to pursue the steps outlined in Appendix 12-A at the end of Chapter Twelve.

141. All three personality aspects have both good and bad sides.
142. The three aspects of personality drive partners' communications without their adequate awareness and sensitivity and thus both partners get offended during this process quite often. Therefore, it may help our relationships, and life as a whole, if we learn to gauge and adjust the volume of these personality aspects regularly.
143. Overall, understanding the properties of our personality aspects and their balance is quite important for both self-awareness and improving our relationships. Therefore, a quick review of these three aspects of personality is offered in Appendix 12-A. It will help gauge our personal choices, especially for building our relationships. Those discussions elaborate on the above facts about 'personality aspects' too.
144. We can make the following hypotheses about individuals' personality:
    - Self is driven mostly by their instincts and spirit.
    - Ego is driven mostly by their genetics, chemistry, and nervous system. However, Ego is also affected by conditioning and defence mechanisms.
    - Model is driven mostly by conditioning and defence mechanisms as well as social environment.
    - 'Human nature' is mostly a combination of Self and that part of Ego that is driven by genetics, chemistry, and nervous system.
    - All three personality aspects, i.e., Self, Ego, Model, draw on person's cognition (logic) to manage a person's affairs

145. Therefore, personality can be identified and measured in terms of how effectively a person can:
    - apply his/her **instincts (Self)**,
    - reason and use his/her **logic**,
    - connect with people and society—**Model**, and
    - manage his **Ego** for his/her own benefit.

146. A unique mix of the above four factors makes up a person's personality and determines his effectiveness and charisma.
147. The personality aspects, i.e., Self, Model, and Ego, reflect how we value and use the four personality factors, i.e., our instincts, logic, adaptability (model), and ego.
148. For building an ideal relationship, partners should be *good and enlightened* persons first.
149. Being a 'good' person mostly refers to individual's personality dominance. Obviously, the more a partner is driven by Self, and the less he/she is influenced by Ego, the better he/she is, with a higher chance to build an ideal relationship. Goodness is a reflection of a person's level of naturalness and integrity.
150. However, in reality, most people are becoming more crooked, phony, spoiled, and demanding every day. As a result, they become more incompatible with one another. Personality flaws, insecurities, and evilness reduce the chances of success for relationships drastically.
151. Obviously, genetics determines a good portion of our personality and destiny. Even our conscious attempts to adjust our personality cannot override the effect of genetics
152. People also perceive the world and people according to their unique personalities. The effect of our perception and misperceptions on our relationships are tremendous as discussed in Chapter Seven.
153. Furthermore, it appears that men and women have major differences in terms of perceiving events and people. Each gender has a rather uniform way of interpreting the world and setting its priorities.
154. Nevertheless, it appears that our destinies are largely mapped for us in our genes. We think and act in certain ways that finally lead to a certain destiny.
155. However, we can strengthen our personality and character through self-awareness and by learning about the roles of our three personality aspects in our thoughts, feelings and

actions. We can play an effective role in strengthening both our personality and the health of our relationships.

Chapter Four
Love and Happiness

Love and happiness are two precious attributes that we humans seek obsessively. In fact, we believe love brings us eternal happiness automatically. Furthermore, we have come to believe that love is the most reliable factor for the success of relationships. Thus, we have conditioned our brains, in recent decades, to put too much value and trust in love. We also imagine everybody can feel and find love easily and naturally. Accordingly, our expectations for love and happiness have made our relationships illogically too complex, unnatural, and impractical.

156. We look for love and happiness in relationships because we are programmed, instinctually and culturally, to believe that a soul mate can relieve our loneliness and complete our identity. Furthermore, we believe a good companion can *potentially* satisfy a wide range of our personal needs, including sex, compassion, and spiritual (selfless) love.
157. In a sense, we intuitively put too much faith in the vast potentials of companionship. Accordingly, we remain too naive about the likelihood of turning all that potentiality into reality—to make all those goods things happen.

158. Nevertheless, the outcome is that we seek love and happiness obsessively. Even worse, we hope to find them externally, in our relationships, instead of looking for them within ourselves as a personal challenge.
159. We have not been able to be happy as individuals and we do not know anything about the path to happiness either, so we look for a relationship to do it for us. However, a 'relationship' is not a happiness-generating machine. Thus, we end up placing high expectations on our partners to make the relationship work and make us happy.
160. We make our partners accountable for the happiness that a relationship is supposed to provide. Since our partners are looking for the same thing, our relationships begin to face a great deal of pressure quickly. Instead of getting the kind of happiness we desire, we face our partners' demands to focus on making them happy—a total contrast to what we had initially assumed!
161. We ignore the high likelihood that our partners have not been able to make themselves happy (even though nowadays everybody likes to shout how happy and mature they are and how beautiful life is). So how can we expect them to make us happy? Are we naïve, or selfishly assume we can tame them to serve us?
162. Therefore, partners end up playing all kinds of games and roles to manipulate and control each other, to feel loved and in charge of the relationship in hopes of finding some relative happiness.
163. Of course, sometimes, one partner submits to the whims of the other partner eventually, because he/she gets tired of fighting or playing games, or whatever. However, this type of relationship is doomed and unacceptable in our modern societies anyway.
164. Happiness is a myth all by itself, but finding it in relationships is plain utopian—only a wishful thinking cultivated in our imaginations.

165. A major problem is that we want happiness to fit our contaminated lifestyles, instead of a lifestyle that could induce peace of mind as the closest state of happiness.
166. Unfortunately, human nature does not support happiness and tranquility, either, because of innate human urges for challenge, controversy, power, domination, competition, greed, struggle for survival, etc. Anger, hatred, jealousy, spite, and aggressiveness come to us so naturally, but we must try really hard to be honest, compassionate, sincere, etc.
167. Most relationships become instable soon enough, only because they fail to satisfy our fantastic desires for happiness and sexuality.
168. The slogan 'life's purpose is to find happiness' is in fact causing more suffering than guiding people toward happiness. The reason is that it makes people believe that such a myth (happiness) actually exists, and it is due to their stupidity or relationships they cannot find it.
169. The purpose of life is neither to find and spread happiness, nor to create good human beings. Life does not have any particular meaning, nor is it about anything in particular. Life is merely a collection of events and moments that transpires in people's lives according to natural laws and chances and affects them based on their cognition.
170. Humans have many other ambitions in life, which they often pursue with greater passion than their desire for happiness or even pleasures, e.g., need for love, power, or recognition. Most people just cannot sit idle and be happy with their contentment.
171. Happiness and goodness are the likely outcomes of our choices to set the right balance between our ambitions and contentment.
172. The fact that we have to try so hard to become better human beings and find happiness is another clue that humans are not pure by nature.

173. The simple fact that Ego is an inherent part of the human psyche is enough to cause human bias, selfishness, hypocrisy, and hundreds of other impurities and flaws.
174. Human purity is not a matter of comparing the number of good deeds versus bad ones either, even if people did more good than bad. Purity is an absolute fact and not an algebraic equation. It either exists or does not. The only question is how often humans' impurity approaches evilness. Too often and universally, it usually feels!
175. Propagating that humans are good by nature would only create a false expectation in society, and people get even more disappointed and frustrated regularly when facing reality. The more we consider people's malice unnatural, the more deliberate their actions appear.
176. On the other hand, if we accept that humans are flawed and impure by nature, we would develop more tolerance and compassion, because we understand that human actions are mostly beyond their control or are pushed by greed and social corruption. We might even smarten up and correct the social causes of human corruption.
177. Our reaction to people's claims of purity and happiness shows our major scepticism. We need a lot of evidence to believe in even one person's goodness and happiness.
178. Once we accept that human nature is impure, we would also keep our expectations from people and relationships low. We get less surprised and angry while we develop some form of understanding and compassion toward our partners and the helpless humanity.
179. Nevertheless, we create deep conflicts in our relationships by our faulty assumption that happiness is something that someone else can bring to us. With this kind of mindset, we should expect only more conflicts in our relationships and life in general. Instead of love and happiness, we should expect antagonism and depression as natural traits of humans.

180. Another misunderstanding is that relationships can solve our personal problems, which would then lead to happiness. This is a false assumption and an invalid expectation.
181. Actually, instead of expecting relationships to solve our problems, we should expect and prepare ourselves to deal with the added hardships of relationships and the high likelihood of separation with huge hassles of its own.
182. All the facts, trends, and choices noted in this book clearly demonstrate the need to tame our needs for love and happiness, and instead focus on building teamwork and tolerance for maintaining a sensible relationship.
183. Even when both partners have good intentions, are good-natured, and realize that give and take in a relationship may provide a relative sense of comfort (not necessarily happiness) for both partners, they still do not know how to do it. They do not know how to *relate* fairly.
184. Therefore, we need a *relationship framework* and a set of *principles* to show how partners may relate with the least amount of frictions.
185. This relationship framework and a set of principles must show couples how to maintain a simple relationship without putting too much demand on each other for irrelevant and impossible objectives.
186. These principles and relationship framework must bring objectivity back into relationships.
187. Whether we can find happiness in relationships or not depends on many factors, mainly our mental capacity to interpret, absorb, and reflect happiness. As a first step, we must admit that happiness is more a subjective perception than a tangible commodity to expect from relationships.
188. People behave neurotically and randomly to find happiness in a variety of things or events, like going to yoga, travelling, shopping excessively, looking for love, dancing, getting into art, etc. However, these random searches for relief or happiness might cause only more frustration until we set-

tle with our inner selves, grasp a realistic meaning for happiness, and relax naturally.
189. In fact, our efforts for finding love and happiness often cause extra burden and disappointment that result in only a higher sense of loneliness and failure.
190. Partners' personality affect their perceptions of love and the way they try to satisfy them. In fact, three types of love satisfy the three aspects of our personality:
- **SLove** is Self driven and reflects the most spiritual and selfless way of loving someone.
- **ELove** is Ego driven and reflects our insecurities and deficiency need for love and attention.
- **MLove** is Model driven and reflects our most practical way of communicating our passion to another person without going overboard with some imaginary perceptions about the power of love and its importance for the success of our relationships.

191. People's uniqueness in using their three personality aspects (Ego, Model, and Self) make them perceive 'love' also uniquely in their own ways and react to it differently too.
192. The commonplace love consists of i) physical attraction and lust, and ii) a combination of the three types of love (SLove, MLove, and ELove). Accordingly, we can say that:
- Seeking love reflects both our instinctual and conditional urges.
- A person's 'need for a companion' reflects all three personality aspects (Ego, Model, and Self), which play their roles when someone expresses love to another per-
- The meaning of love is different for each person depending on the level of Ego, Model, and Self he/she has applied to perceive love. Accordingly, each person is driven by a certain level of SLove, MLove, and ELove at the time he/she expresses his/her love.

- Inventing an imaginary meaning for love (outside the meanings of SLove, ELove, MLove) and spreading it for common use is pointless—except for writing fiction and making movies.

193. On most occasions, our initial perception and impression of SLove fades away after we get into relationships. The reason is very simple: Self is needed to protect SLove. Besides, SLove deteriorates when partners' new perceptions about their relationship override their initial ones.
194. The complex 'need for a companion' comprises of many personal needs that extend over the full spectrum of 'personal needs tree,' from the basic need for sex all the way to our high-level need for spirituality through SLove.
195. The main urges that drive humans to find a mate are Sex, Compassion, and SLove. Compassion by itself includes many other urges such as ELove, MLove, security, dependence, respect, and recognition.
196. Naively, we assume that our partners are capable of satisfying the whole spectrum of our needs, including sex, compassion, and love, and thus make us happy.
197. In reality, however, even the task of satisfying sex in relationships has become rather complex, because, sex is often treated nowadays as a regulating tool to tame our partners, instead of a basic need.
198. Furthermore, sexual deprivations have risen due to couples' drive for ELove (deficiency love) getting out of control.
199. With regard to compassion, couples are also lacking the required qualities to satisfy this complex need of humans. In fact, the supply and demand for compassion is imbalanced. People demand a lot of compassion from their relationships, but hardly have any themselves to share with their partners; or do not know how to go about showing it.
200. Both our basic need for sex (including the urge for reproduction, especially for women) and our high-level need for

love (SLove) are instinctual needs. Therefore, it appears that we have created most of the medium-range personal needs (including compassion) through evolution and according to cultural conditions. Therefore, the need for compassion has become quite complex to understand and satisfy too.

201. Nevertheless, our challenge in relationships is to learn about sharing compassion without imagining and expecting it as a requirement, especially in terms of SLove (selfless love).

202. In terms of satisfying the personal need for love, we have the hardest time. While all kind of ambiguity and complication surround the matter of love, our drive to find happiness through love is tough to curtail.

203. Yet, we cannot stop our search for that special person who can make our dreams come true. We hope to complete our existence through him/her. This crusade is partly the symptom of people's instinctual need for spiritual love (SLove) —the selfless kind of love that falls at the highest level of human needs tree. However, we are mostly seeking ELove (deficiency love)—the selfish need to be loved by someone who solves our insecurities too.

204. People have the following motives for expressing or expecting love: (See the details in Appendix 4-A at the end of this chapter.)
- To *communicate* with their partners.
- To express their basic *feelings*.
- To release *psychological* pressures.
- To mimic their *spiritual* needs.
- To *control* their partners.
- To *manipulate* (abuse) their partners.

205. Love has become such a precious commodity nowadays, because it can satisfy a variety of personal needs and motives. However, while people seek love to share a spiritual experience with their soul mate, many people are inherently

incapable of giving love. They merely want to be loved to heal their insecurities and to control their partners.

206. Accordingly, need for control, possessiveness, and jealousy are not the reflections of true love. They only represent a person's rampant emotions and the urge to control others for ELove, money, friendship, sex, etc.

207. Many people do not have the patience or time even for a simple friendship, but still insist on building a 'love' relationship. They disregard the basic principles, such as courtesy and respect, to allow their friendship grow in a natural way. Instead, they depend on their weird games to incite a phony love. How can people trust each other for a serious relationship if they do not even know how to be good friends?

208. The main feature of successful friendships, which is missing in relationships, is that friends' limited expectations come naturally, without pressure or demand. Then even if those expectations are not fulfilled, they usually do not argue or fight, but rather moderate their own expectations to sustain their friendship.

209. The meaning of the word 'love' has become too ambiguous and arbitrary due to many facts explained in this book, including individuals' unique needs and perceptions about love.

210. On the other hand, since love has become the locus of relationships in modern societies, we must at least know what it is and understand the role it can realistically play in relationships.

211. Accordingly, to appreciate love and possibly enjoy it, we should remove the ambiguities surrounding our present impression of it. Therefore, the following definitions might further clarify some of our misperceptions about love.

212. The word 'love,' in the context used nowadays, consists of people's impression (and expression) of their 1) urges, 2) feelings, and 3) moods during their search for a companion.

213. The **Urges** are mostly sexual, but also driven by loneliness, insecurity, need for belonging, etc.
214. The **Feelings** related to humans' search for a mate are numerous, including delight, elation, lust, jealousy, possessiveness, hatred, anger, and all other feelings that humans face while chasing any desire. A variety of feelings emerges during their love related affairs, success, or failure.
215. The **Moods** that emerge during humans' search for a companion are comprised of: Attraction, Romance, and Attachment. They evolve from a mix of urges and feelings, but also by our conscious assessment of the person we feel attracted to.
216. **Attraction** is triggered by physical appeal, lust, but also our careful evaluation of a person's qualities and resources. Our instinctual criteria for selecting a mate, mostly for the purpose of bearing a child with this person, often play their role too.
217. **Romance** is our innate impression of SLove and our calculating expressions of passion in order to lure in our beloved. Therefore, again, we are using both our instinctual and logical assets to find a companion.
218. **Attachment** is the effect of closeness to a person and enjoying the compassion satisfied by this union.
219. We have historically combined all these urges, feelings, and moods and called it love, thus creating such a vague definition to deal with.
220. People suffer because of love for two main reasons: First, the forces behind their love urges, feelings, and moods are not clear to them in order to deal with the sources of their anxieties directly. Second, they assume love is a lasting condition.
221. Understanding the true meaning and implications of love might help us curb our initial unwarranted enthusiasm and prepare ourselves better for its heartbreaking consequences.

222. The *urges, moods, and feelings* related to 'finding a companion' should be studied as psychological reactions—symptoms of love—but not love itself.

223. True love is that one instinctual urge that we have identified as SLove. Love, in its purest sense, is just a simple, selfless appreciation for the mere 'being' of another person without having any selfish urges to own, control, or impose one's needs upon that person.

224. This pure feeling of SLove, which is engraved in our unconscious, is occasionally directed toward our beloved, too, but usually for a short period. This is because we usually have a hard time internalizing SLove unless we learn to become a selfless individual.

225. We create all kinds of images and love moods (in the form of attraction and romance) in our minds when some flickers of SLove strike us. However, these love moods are the outcome of our urgent urges for 'sex' and 'compassion,' as we struggle to find a companion.

226. Overall, it is our strong 'need for a companion' (once directed toward a particular person) that creates all those urges, feelings, and moods that we customarily (and wrongly) attribute to love.

227. This subtle understanding about love is important because it makes us think and put our love related urges and feelings into a proper perspective. We remember that merely our 'need for a companion' and 'sense of loneliness' often make us behave in strange ways.

228. Furthermore, we should realize that the real cause of our restlessness and loneliness is not love (or lack of it), although we crave more love the lonelier we get. The real cause of our loneliness is our rising inability to *relate* to one another, while our obsession to find a soul mate keeps growing at the same time.

229. This awareness might goad us to adopt a new mentality: to either give less importance to having a companion, or go

about finding him/her in a more honest, productive, and natural manner.

230. Our 'need for a *dependable* companion' is actually so impaired it has turned into '*desperation* for a companion' in recent decades.

231. Yet, we remain hopeful all our lives to find a soul mate who would fulfil most of our personal needs.

232. Realistically, however, our chances for actually finding a soul mate is quite remote, and then realizing the 'potentialities' of a companion (and maintaining good relationships) has even a lower chance for all the reasons enumerated in this book.

233. Nowadays, partners have difficulty even fulfilling each other's basic need for sex on a long-term basis, let alone all those more complex needs for ELove, compassion, and SLove.

234. Yet, people seem to have a chronic optimism about the potentialities of relationships despite their repeated failures, frustration, anger, and desperation.

235. Our desperation for a companion would keep rising because we cannot maintain a relationship or trust our partners in the long run.

236. A major problem is that we have become too idealistic. Instead of understanding the roots of relationship problems and our role in causing many of them, we keep dreaming about a soul mate and an ideal relationship with another partner. We do not see the futility of our search for love or a soul mate.

237. Naturally, the more relationships fail, the more desperate people get, which ironically only heightens their craving for love even more. It is easy to notice that the more a person is desperate to find a companion, the faster and deeper he/she falls in love.

238. In all, our obsession for love nowadays is a reflection of our loneliness and desperation for a companion, but our exag-

gerated expectations (including love) ruin our relationships and we become even more desperate and lonely. This vicious cycle is destroying people's trust in one another and their expressions of love.

239. If we realize that love cannot be the success factor for relationships, we might decide to reassess and revamp our own personalities, lifestyles, needs, demands, and methods of going about finding a companion.

240. The way we have become—so haughty and oversensitive—is to be blamed for the failure of relationships, not the lack of love or couple's inability to be romantic.

241. **Attraction** has been a rather instinctual mood (process) for selecting a mate going back millions of years in the history of evolution. Nowadays we get attracted, or pretend to be attracted, to someone based on many other factors, too, such as his/her wealth, social standing, ambition, appearance, etc. Thus, the purity of attraction is questionable nowadays.

242. **Romance** has always existed in nature, too, yet its role has also been tentative (like 'Attraction') for both animals and humans. However, we like to have lots of it nowadays—a naive demand that is increasing expectations and clashes when couples cannot deliver romance naturally on a regular basis.

243. **Attachment** has evolved in humans as the need for support to raise offspring emerged for our ancestors many millenniums ago. It was mostly a temporary arrangement, too, and then partners felt independent again when children could live on their own.

244. Nowadays we have gotten used to the idea of having a long-term commitment with a partner. Aside from historical, religious, and ethical influence, this new mentality has grown stronger as humans have become more insecure, calculating, and needy for love and compassion in recent history.

245. At the same time, we have become too arrogant and demanding, and thus sabotage our chances to sustain long commitments with anybody.
246. Nonetheless, our yearning for both romance and attachment appears to be largely self-imposed moods and also a reflection of humans' struggle for social morality.
247. Love has always been addressed as a combination of many feelings, urges, and moods related to humans' search for a companion. If the ancient Greek had defined ten different kinds of love, now psychologist come up with six or eight types again based on its symptoms.
248. However, dividing love into certain categories by attaching certain feelings to each category would not help the existing chaos in relationships. It only convolutes the meaning of a simple concept like love even more.
249. In the final analysis, the essence of love is always that notion of selflessness toward another being regardless of all the feelings and urges that are manifesting in that particular case, e.g., love toward our children, parents, a person, or even objects such as Nature, artistic passion, etc. Love is always the unique feeling of SLove regardless of all the emotions that get attached to it.
250. Sometimes we make a big fuss about the way a lover becomes restless, jealous, depressed, sleepless, etc. However, these symptoms are common in many other situations, too, when any particular plan or desire of a person is threatened. People lose sleep and become restless about any matter that occupies their minds, e.g., a project, a catastrophe, etc., or get jealous if a job promotion is given to another person.
251. The symptoms of love should not affect the nature of love, if it is true love. Even compassion, which is noble and often more precious than even love, should not be mixed up with love.
252. Pure, unselfish SLove satisfies some peaceful emotions and urges of humans, but it does not lead to self-destruction or

war with our beloved. This is the simple definition of love adopted in this book.

253. Hatred and rage, when love fails, clearly show that our perception of 'love' had not been pure (SLove). Obviously, many of our selfish and destructive urges and feelings influence our *impression and expression* of love. Therefore, it helps to know the real motives behind these urges and feelings.

254. In all, people's sense of love nowadays consists of some kind of mixed urges for sex, compassion, and an impression of SLove. Then they express some feelings and moods, all in an attempt to find a companion.

255. Hormones that rule human urges do not seem to support people's excessive expectations from love and relationships. The discussions in Chapter Five about human hormones reveal many other facts.

256. In the past, love had little impact on people's daily lives and their relationships, simply because people did not read many books and were not exposed to such relentless amount of misleading propaganda about love. They had real life hardships to worry about. They were not so obsessed about expressing themselves as much either.

257. The new social values have brainwashed us to make love the locus of relationships and thus inflict enormous pressure upon ourselves and our partners.

258. Love has become confused with attraction and mixed up with many other urges and feelings of humans. The objectives of love and relationships are also muddled up in people's minds in a destructive way.

259. Overall, the destiny of love does not look to be very bright because:
   - The meaning of love is getting more ambiguous and useless, especially for building relationships. However, we usually like to make a big deal about the phrase "I love you." In effect, the use of the word love has become too

hypocritical considering people's varied purposes for, and understanding of, love.
- The general increase in social complexity, sexuality, and corruption makes people less and less trustful of one another and their expressions of love. At the same time, people insist that relationships and love must be built on absolute trust and honesty.

260. Our limited options to face the reality of love and relationships are:
- To become selfless and internalize SLove,
- To pursue love affairs here and there if we are lucky,
- To live alone while waiting for love,
- To use MLove to instil mutual respect and civility in relationships.

261. Using MLove in relationships has other advantages too: It provides a venue for partners to be romantic without raising relationship expectations or creating misunderstandings about their love expressions.

262. Another advantage of MLove is that expressing one's feelings through MLove would partially respond to partners' need for SLove.

263. MLove also fulfils some of partners' ELove needs. This happens because people's *subconscious* can easily substitute MLove for ELove, while their *conscious* minds remember the purpose of MLove.

264. MLove is a voluntary and possibly periodical gesture by one or both partners. A partner should not turn it into an expectation; otherwise, it would be ELove and not MLove anymore.

265. Overall, love has no real meaning to draw upon or set expectations for. We can use it arbitrarily only to soothe our need for compassion without making an issue out of it or expecting long-term commitment on that basis. "You said

you loved me!" is a common complaint when couples interpret 'love' based on their random and vague perceptions.

266. Obviously, the word 'love' covers a large variety of meanings and none of them really reflects true love (SLove). This ambiguity and misperception in people's minds cause so much conflict in relationships.

267. Furthermore, 'love' is perceived and applied differently by each individual according to his/her psychological and circumstantial needs.

268. Couples get hurt because of their wrong impressions of love, and because they annoy each other with their exaggerated expectations for love and attention.

269. People destroy not only their chances for building manageable relationships, but also the opportunity of understanding the meaning of SLove.

270. Accordingly, expecting love in relationships or hoping to find happiness through love is a futile dream in general, although a few people can attain all that in certain circumstances, mostly through self-awareness and being a better person themselves.

271. Our culture permeates many invalid myths about love. We believe that:
- Love is the test of success for relationships.
- Love lasts forever.
- Love makes a relationship last forever.
- Relationships must be validated by love.
- Relationships thrive on love.
- Anybody considering a serious relationship should and would find a person to exchange love with each other.
- Expressing love regularly guarantees the success of relationships.
- Love is a common phenomenon that everyone understands and is capable of delivering.

- Love is a common commodity that everyone must find and enjoy in his/her life.
- When there is love, relationship problems are rare and manageable.
- Love overcomes all the relationship problems.
- Partners have control over their feelings to love each other forever.

272. The above myths are furthest from the nature of relationships in the new era. Love does not have the meaning or the power stipulated in the above myths. Nor do relationships necessarily last longer if partners start their relationships with love.
273. We are not learning any lesson from the fact that almost all relationships in the modern world have started based on *some kind of love* and they still keep failing miserably. It is amazing.
274. Nowadays, couples have become both too romantic and antagonistic.
275. Many couples are frustrated and confused, as they feel trapped in their loveless (maybe hostile) relationships. This is especially stressful for those who are adamant that love is the essence of relationships.
276. Hypocrisy and deceit overwhelm our love affairs and relationships when we constantly draw on Model to play games and manipulate our partners.
277. Being natural requires keeping Model at the minimum level needed only for etiquette and tactfulness, before it leads to phoniness. Accordingly, using MLove in our relationships must be sincere and natural to help couples relate and exchange compassion.
278. A simple fact about the meaning of love has been ignored in our new culture: We do not appreciate that the more one seeks SLove, the more one must be honest and sincere in character. Yet we have lost our ability to be natural and sin-

cere because of all the complex games that have been introduced in relationships in recent decades.

279. Like other aspects of social life these days, a superficial (embellished) love is acceptable and preferred to sincerity and reality.

280. Even 'love' is contaminated by selfishness and gross misperceptions nowadays.

281. Partners look for unconditional (selfless) love from each other, but impose many conditions to ensure *equality,* even in terms of the level of love they exchange.

282. While equality, in the sense of *fairness,* is the foundation of democratic societies, the concept of equality has turned into a socio-political platform to further spread our demented social values.

283. The concept of love is often confused in the minds of couples who not only make the equality of love a relationship requirement, but also *retaliate* harshly when their love is not returned equally.

284. We imagine that we can hide our insincerity, mistrust, and dishonesty from the rest of the world. However, this mentality only shows our arrogance and high belief in Model to bail us out. The good news is that people can see each other's true nature despite all the elaborate games they play to pretend a false personality of themselves and to conceal their calculating nature.

285. The games and retaliation schemes in relationships show how ridiculous the idea of measuring the strength of our relationships by 'love' is. We just ignore all these contradictions and keep looking for SLove in such a contaminated environment.

286. Loving someone requires a special knowledge and awareness.

287. For true love, partners need a highly developed character. For example, only a fool might believe in love expressions by a naïve person.

288. The complexity of both love and relationships is evident in the manner couples use Ego, Mode, and Self, to communicate their perceived feelings of love.
289. Since love is, nowadays, the glue that holds couples together, all other aspects of their relationships become difficult to manage and appreciate, as well, when love begins to lose its intensity.
290. Promises and wedding vows actually create many problems in relationships. For one thing, promises raise partners' expectations from each other unrealistically. The main problem, however, is that partners get a wrong impression about the security and permanence of their relationship. They ignore that all relationships are vulnerable and require constant attention and work in order to survive one more day.
291. What we call love in our relationships is often only a combination of lust, possessiveness, and psychological deficiencies we have compiled through social interactions. Besides, not even SLove is necessarily a success factor for relationships anyway.

Appendix 4-A
Personal Needs (Motives) behind Love

We exchange love (mostly ELove) to satisfy many personal needs and motives. Some of these prominent motives are:

- To *communicate* with our partners. Showing passion may be only a means of striking a conversation with our partners for many reasons, maybe for measuring some aspects of the relationship, or possibly even for manipulating our partners.
- To express our basic *feelings*. We may show passion to draw our partners' attention to our urgent needs and feelings. We may feel happy, fulfilled, depressed, lonely, lost, etc. We like to share any kind of feelings with our partners and hope to receive their sympathy too.
- To release *psychological* pressures. We may show passion for satisfying our needs for acceptance and dependence. Insecurity and need for continuous recognition motivate a partner to use ELove as a mechanism to enforce his/her dependency on his/her partner.
- To mimic our *spiritual* needs. We have an instinctual urge for SLove. Although our medium range needs prevent us from acting on this high-level need, SLove is triggered subconsciously now and then, e.g., when we hear a romantic tune or watch a drama. For a moment, we get in touch with this obscure feeling, i.e., SLove. We may eventually act upon it, but usually these spiritual experiences are fleeting moments that we cannot internalize and apply regularly. As noted before, SLove happens only after fulfilling (or containing) our basic and medium needs and becoming a needless and selfless person. This spiritual love requires these levels of maturity and enlightenment.
- To *control* our partners. An inconspicuous, but common, purpose of love is to satisfy one's need for control. That is,

often, a person's urge for love is for the purpose of controlling his/her partner somewhat easier. People exchange love phrases, hoping to enhance their partners' love for them, so that they can live within certain boundaries agreeable to one or both partners, depending on who loves the other more and who is setting the boundaries. People's rising urge for control is not always out of malice. They do it because that is the only method they know for managing their relationships and for prolonging them. Another reason for partners' 'need for control' is that they trust each other less every day and thus get an urge to impose controls on each other.

- To *manipulate (abuse)* our partners. Sometimes a partner expresses love or attachment only for (ab)using his/her partner—mostly for his/her personal financial and sexual needs—with the least amount of sincerity in his/her words or attitude.

Chapter Five
Hormones and Gender Differences

Gender differences and hormones are two other factors causing severe relationship conflicts and reducing partners' ability to connect. This chapter discusses only some of the primary facts about gender differences, hormones, and their symptoms in relationships. Chapter Eleven offers another hundred relationship trends caused by gender differences. Another book in this series is planned to discuss these topics exclusively in more details.

With regard to hormones, scientists have reached the following conclusions:

292. Sexual activity triggers the mood for cuddling and attachment, but the increased sex might erode the sense of attachment in the long run.
293. Although attachment might increase sexual urge initially, prolonged attachment might eventually dampen the urge for sex.
294. Romance and attachment are not proven to be related.
295. Attachment might erode romance.
296. Romance might erode sex.

297. Humans are not built to be monogamous, unlike some animals that have the right chemistry for it.
298. Love dies most likely within six months to about two years.
299. Humans are chemically (instinctually) inclined to connect to different people for satisfying different urges (romance, sex, attachment).
300. The effect of human hormones and mood changes, especially for women during childbirth, menstrual cycle, and menopause, make the effect of gender differences even more prominent.

With respect to gender differences due to hormonal, conditional, or other factors, the following points are observed:

301. While both genders have equal sexual drives, they often have different motives for acting upon it.
302. Women's natural superiority in creating and safeguarding their offspring appears to contribute to the fact that men lose their priority in relationships when children are born.
303. Another outer force affecting relationships adversely without anyone's fault is that women are in a state of transition in terms of the progressive role they would like to play in society and relationships.
304. Women's new role in relationships is not understood even by the majority of women, let alone by men who are expected to not only know what the new format should be, but also respond positively too.
305. A special situation seems to have emerged: Due to men's passivity, women find it necessary to become aggressive in order to attain the assertiveness they need urgently.
306. It would be an inherently difficult task, for men especially, to achieve the changes required in terms of gender roles, even in a timelier manner, even if they agreed to the changes women are asking.

307. Within this confusing and stressful situation, all kinds of destructive aggressions by both men and women are convoluting the transition process. Instead of progress, we witness more sabotage, retaliation, games, divorces, and family murder suicides.
308. The bottom line is that men have lost their identity (whatever it was, good or bad) and do not understand the sensibility of what is expected of them. And women are frustrated, too, because they cannot prove and enforce a new identity, which they believe they know what it is.
309. The result of the current confusion (about gender identities) is that partners finally get fed up with their struggles to convince each other logically. Therefore, they try to dominate each other or resort to divorce.
310. What works for women in a relationship does not work for men anymore, and vice versa. In particular, men and women mistrust the opposite genders much more than their own. The increasing same-sex relationships *might be* partly due to the fact that they get along better.
311. It appears that we are reaching an era where men can no longer be what women want (in terms of character) and vice versa.
312. In all, both genders and all couples are facing a confusing transition period.
313. The transition period mainly refers to the process of men and women learning their relationship roles in the new era. However, in reality, it refers to the long period for couples, especially women, to realize that their expectations from relationships are not logical and feasible.
314. People, especially women, are nowadays too idealistic, ambitious, neurotic, and stressed out due to their new lifestyles and fantasies.
315. Women make a lot of fuss about their need for independence, but also demand to be spoiled. Ironically, they do not see the conflict either.

316. Many people, especially women, take the flattery they receive a sign of their chances to find a better mate once they leave their present partners. Then after separation, they realize how they have been misled.
317. People, especially men, are enjoying the present situation with multiple dating and all, while they (mostly women) are getting more frustrated due to their failure to find a qualified partner and also facing their mates' (mostly men's) rising passivity.
318. Men and women are so incompatible in general that when, by chance, they match and really love one another for a long time, it appears like a magical and spiritual sensation beyond our normal (expected) worldly experiences. It is such an odd event and coincidence. Still we naïvely believe love should happen to all of us and thus we seek it like a reasonable expectation.
319. The increasing rivalry and clashes between men and women look like some kind of all out gender warfare. The level of insults, belittling, retaliations, intimidations, abuse, manipulation, badmouthing, power struggles, competition, crying, making a scene, screaming, blackmailing, and trying to outsmart one another just keep increasing.
320. Men and women are becoming increasingly alienated due to the changing social values and couples' drive to establish their gender identities better (usually at the cost of weakening the other gender's identity). It appears that some inherent gender differences are also adding fuel to the matter of couples' alienation in relationships.
321. Many of the clashes between men and women are due to women's higher instinctual tendency challenging men's higher logical predisposition.
322. In reality, however, both our instincts and logic are usually flawed anyway. Therefore, often, nobody is right due to their erroneous perceptions and lack of objectivity.

323. Then problems increase because men and women want to change each other's decision processes, i.e., to make them more logical or intuitive—more like themselves. They fail because the instinctual urges of women and the logical tendencies of men are too deep to change quickly even if they realized the need for it. Their inherent personality traits often hinder this change to happen.
324. Women have a harder time in satisfying their conflicting needs for dependence and independence than men do. This is due to the emphasis nowadays for women to seek independence as a means of establishing their identity. This pressure aggravates their already conflicting (instinctual) urges for both dependence and independence.
325. Instinctually, women seek security and dependence more than men do. For example, women are more eager to find love and a social partner, because they not only are more optimistic about the possibility of finding their soul mates, but also crave love harder instinctually—due to their higher urges for reproduction, social adaptation (Model), and socializing. In addition, their exaggerated show of, and search for, independence hinders the natural fulfilment of their need for dependence. Accordingly, the more independence they acquire, the more they feel deprived of satisfying their urge for dependence.
326. Therefore, women are facing a big dilemma nowadays: On the one hand, they like to depend on men, for procreation and for fulfilling their higher social needs due to their higher Model. On the other hand, they feel the urgency to assert their identity by proving their independence. This dilemma creates inner conflict and confusion for them and widens the gender gap too. They often do not accept or feel this inner conflict, but most likely struggle with it subconsciously.
327. Seeking more independence is also a matter of 'life phase' for women, while raising and enjoying their kids. They feel empowered and independent due to their maternal power,

but also because they presume their men are sticking around for emergencies anyway. Once their kids are gone, however, their need for dependence takes precedence again, especially if men have strayed.

328. Inherently, women need dependence on men also for general support and completing their social identity, though they prefer to hide this fact.

329. Men's inner conflict in terms of dependence/independence is rather straightforward and much simpler. They seek independence instinctually, but need to depend on women to fulfil some of their basic needs, including compassion and sex. They appear helpless without women for managing their daily routines, while inherently they continue to value their own independence highly.

330. Therefore, while both genders drive for both dependence and independence regularly, they do so for completely different reasons. Furthermore, they go through this cycle even more forcefully at some stages of their relationships. They start a relationship to fulfil their need for dependence (mostly their basic needs, e.g., sex and ELove). Soon, however, they take their relationship for granted and press for a complex need like independence (according to their naïve perceptions of, and unique needs for, independence.)

Many other points (over 100) about the implications of gender differences in relationships are discussed in Chapter Eleven where relationship trends are discussed. Those trends reflect men's and women's peculiar viewpoints about their relationships and the new ways they behave toward one another. Nevertheless, those trends are symptoms of the emerging or inherent gender differences that could have been listed in this chapter as new facts evolving in relationships.

Chapter Six
Social Environment and Values

In recent decades, our relationships have shaped too closely around social environment and values, which merely propagate superficiality and arrogance. Therefore, the form and characteristics of relationships nowadays are not in line with humans' natural needs and capacities. Instead, we have created a social structure and relationship mishmash that is incapable of serving either humans or a civilized society. Especially, with women's new role in society and the decline of religious influence, we have developed many idiotic roles and demands in relationships. Some of the effects of social environment and values on relationships are explained in the following pages.

331. People are getting more insecure due to our crooked social structure and values and thus they have become needier for attention and love. When they do not get it at the desired level, they feel even more lost and lonely.
332. Relationships have become too important nowadays because people's basic needs, e.g., food and shelter, are easily satisfied in modern societies. With less pressing issues and

hardship that most people around the world must face, we luckier humans fuss too much about love and happiness.

333. Relationships appear like the best antidote for loneliness, too, because we cannot live independently anymore despite all our pretensions for individualism and freedom.

334. At the same time, providing constant attention to our insecure partners is a major responsibility that causes anxiety besides all the extra work needed for running our careers, relationships, and other family affairs.

335. Furthermore, our accurate view of corruption and duplicity in society cause cynicism about people's truthfulness and authenticity.

336. A major hurdle in relationships is that people trust one another less every day due to bad personal experiences and rampant socioeconomic corruption in modern societies.

337. On the other hand, the high percentage of marriage breakdowns and subsequent headaches make relationships too risky nowadays. So absolute caution regarding the words and promises of our partners is warranted.

338. The cost (consequences) of trusting our partners is high because they usually disappoint us sooner or later. However, the cost of not showing full trust in them is also too high, as they find it insulting and a sign of our indifference toward them. This inevitable dilemma and our doubtfulness put extra pressure on couples and their relationships.

339. Many humble individuals are out there who could be in good relationships together if they were not deterred by their (often justified) paranoia about the state of relationships and their lack of trust in people.

340. Mistrust is a natural (and often necessary) condition in relationships in the new era. This is a logical consequence of social life and not a sign of a person's weakness or selfishness.

341. Eliminating or overcoming the causes of mistrust in relationships is almost impossible, too, because they are only

symptoms of new social structure that advocates greed, arrogance, and materialism.

342. However, people's mistrust is often also caused by their own oversensitivity and misperceptions, which then affects their behaviour and their partners' added mistrust in them. In all, partners must remain conscious of the high possibility and causes of misjudging each other.

343. We should not expect our partners to trust us completely, especially when we feel the difficulty of trusting them completely ourselves.

344. We can never know *who we are* or *who they are* and they can never know *who they are* or *who we are*. We must honour these two facts with open minds. We struggle all our lives to find ourselves and happiness, to no avail. So, how can we expect others to know us and trust us when even we do not? It is simply impossible to build trust based on our doubtful perceptions of ourselves and others.

345. We all rather know that our primary (premarital) impressions of our partners are not necessarily true and complete. So our inherent mistrust is partly due to our wisdom about the high likelihood that the real character of a person often manifests only after some, or years of, cohabitation.

346. We should not consider love and trust as main factors of relationships' health anymore. These are misleading, illogical yardsticks. People often lie about their love or trust to avoid confrontations, or to be tactful and wise. Furthermore, demanding trust or love beyond people's natural capacity would only bring more duplicity and phoniness into relationships.

347. Deep down, we know that couples' promises or commitments are not reliable. Especially, taking the phrase 'I love you' seriously, as a sign of commitment, is naïve.

348. We must come to terms with two major facts in the new era: 1) it is natural that partners lose trust in each other to some extent eventually, and 2) we should learn to live in relation-

ships with imperfect trust levels instead of making a big issue about it. We should be ultra cautious at the time of starting our relationships, but then remain flexible about the inevitable mistrust and disappointments later on.
349. Of course, building this type of mentality is difficult. Thus, a new relationship framework and set of principles must be propagated in society gradually.
350. People do not know how to be tactful or observe even simple etiquettes, but keep insisting on the purity of their soul.
351. While everybody is obsessed about finding his/her soul mate, the chance of it ever happening is slim. However, we all have difficulty accepting this fact, since we want to stay positive and sociable. Our romantic search for a soul mate is preventing us from perceiving relationships realistically.
352. Relationships also force lifestyle changes and adaptation, often for tolerating our partner's idiosyncrasies and fitting with our partners' family habits and conflicting preferences.
353. However, instead of learning about the ways to adapt ourselves for new relationship environment, we try to push our outmoded mentalities and methods.
354. All along, we struggle and hope to change our partner to fit our needs and make our relationship prosper. Stubbornly, we see no need for changing any of our own attitude and values.
355. Hope is an innate urge that keeps us motivated in our boring lives, but it must not make us dogmatic, e.g., about finding love in our relationships or the possibility of making our partner change their attitude. Hope is a useful urge for survival but not a reliable decision factor.
356. Nevertheless, people do not change unless they feel the need for it through years of meditation and self-awareness, mainly for personal goals and not somebody else's, e.g. his/her marriage partner. Therefore, partners' retaliations and intimidations to change each other are just a reflection of their own naivety.

357. In our present convoluted environment, most often partners actually end up ruining each other's lives instead of enriching it. This is because life is getting more complex and stressful every year and people have more difficulty coping with social pressures while they live longer too. People are too stressed and impatient to handle their excessive relationship demands effectively.
358. The longer partners stay in a relationship, the more substantial and incompatible their needs for both dependence and independence become. Accordingly, this imbalance increases both the level of personal inner conflicts and the pressure placed on their relationship.
359. The more complex our societies and interactions get, the more we feel a need to control the sources of potential threats to our physical and mental welfare, including our partners. This is particularly true because nowadays we trust people much less than we did even a few decades ago.
360. We never recognize the source of our crooked behaviour, or we deny its destructive force and impact on our relationships. However, even if we accept our flaws, we can hardly do much about them.
361. The scars, hurt feelings, and bad experiences cannot be forgotten easily. Their deep effect can always be traced in our personality and unexpected aggression, hatred, and self-pity.
362. External (outer) forces, e.g., Nature, society, economy, and work environment, influence our mood and reaction to events regularly. Accordingly, they affect our long-term view of life and our relationships.
363. External forces turn into either *conditional* or *reactional* forces within each person.
364. Conditional forces are those personal habits and values that we have adopted wholeheartedly, like greed and arrogance. They are the absorbed effects of *external forces*.

365. Conditional forces severely influence couples' perceptions and priorities in relationships. And, together with the effect of genetics, they make the likelihood of partners' compatibility very remote.
366. Conditional forces also entail our doubts, quirks, and insecurities.
367. Reactional forces (defence mechanisms), such as anger and retaliation, reside in our unconscious and subconscious minds and then suddenly activate our nervous system with a strong blow.
368. Obviously, under the hostile environment of relationships, each one of us turns into another destructive *external force* for our partners.
369. A great deal of anger and stress is out there in society due to people's inability to find a suitable companion or enjoy their existing relationships. Partners just keep arguing and blaming each other's lack of common sense to understand their seemingly justified needs.
370. At the same time, the rising level of stress in society has made us vulnerable and too needy for sympathy, but there is nobody out there to give it to us.
371. Couples' ability to give and receive compassion in their relationships depends on how humble and enlightened they really are.
372. As a practical step, partners should begin to realize that nowadays the sense of commitment is vastly eroded by the need for individualism.
373. Due to our high expectations from life nowadays, and positive thinking, we always imagine that we can find (or could have found) a better partner than the one we have. We believe we deserve a better one and that he/she can be found if we look around for him/her. However, any seeming desirable partner proves inadequate again soon enough.

374. Thus, for relative tranquility, we must ultimately learn the art of living independently instead of looking for a soul mate to bring us happiness.
375. Nevertheless, we always face a major dilemma (trade off) in life: companionship brings us headaches, and tranquility requires loneliness and self-reliance. The question is how to choose the best option for us according to our personality.
376. Of course, the ultimate question is whether we can develop relationship models for the new era, which fit couples' personalities and provide an atmosphere for a relatively tranquil and effective companionship. This author believes that this option is plausible if we develop a relationship framework and its corresponding principles to bring objectivity back into relationships.
377. With the constant increase of relationship conflicts nowadays, only a proactive (preventative) approach might stop relationship breakdowns. Partners must now foresee and prevent relationship conflicts as much as possible.
378. Instead of depending on partners to imagine the purposes of relationships and behave randomly according to their interpretations, a workable framework based on social conditions of the time must be made available to everybody.
379. We need tools to measure the success of relationships objectively, instead of letting the selfishness and neediness of partners make this critical judgment. Presently, only partners' arrogance is being measured during conflicts, instead of the health of their relationships.
380. Instead of relying on random criteria of couples or their in-laws, an objective set of modest criteria should define the health and success of relationships. In this sense, 'relationships' is viewed as an independent *entity* free from random judgments and perceptions of partners.
381. As we insist on more independence and individualism, the need for teamwork and communication becomes greater for keeping our Egos under a leash.

382. At the same time, for teamwork, partners should have some genuine qualities, including modesty and objectivity. Yet, modesty and the obsession for individualism often do not go together.
383. Overall, we are placing a lot of pressure on society and our partners with our rampant needs for things, sympathy, and security. This attitude and approach is limiting the chances of relationships to pursue a practical path.
384. Someday we must realize and agree that relationship expectations set beyond some modest, humanistic levels are artificial and imposed by psychologically distressed and deprived people. Then, we will rush to redefine relationships as an independent entity with unique needs.
385. The obvious first step for assessing relationship conflicts is to establish whether they are genuine or only created based on partners' exaggerated expectations, unfulfilled personal needs, or idiosyncrasies. However, the question is who would be doing this assessment for couples and society as a whole, and according to what yardsticks? Depending on marriage counsellors have so far failed to achieve lasting solutions for this conundrum.
386. The reality is that before any outsider, including a marriage counsellor, can be of any use, people must learn a variety of new principles about relationships and begin to adjust their mentalities about the purpose of relationships.
387. Too many relationships are nowadays ruined due to partners' subjective assessments and hasty decisions.
388. A simple fact is that the increasing complexity of relationships cannot be handled loosely anymore. It would be too risky to depend on erratic perceptions and interpretations of people to define relationships randomly. We need a rather universal relationship framework.
389. Out of necessity, everybody would realize eventually that relationship decisions must become less arbitrary and emotional.

390. Obviously, couples' unique personalities lead to a large variety of relationship types. Still, it is possible for all of them to work from within a similar framework to maximize relationships' effectiveness. Trusting some generally acceptable norms for assessing our relationships would be preferable to depending on our subjective (and often misleading) views of our relationships.
391. The deep sense of failure to find our soul mate, despite our lifelong search and struggles, causes lasting psychological scars and stress.
392. Therefore, our ultimate objective, as individuals, society, and government should be to bring objectivity back into relationships by advocating a modern relationship framework and a set of relationship principles.
393. Experts suggest all kinds of solutions for relationship problems and still relationships keep failing more than ever. This indicates that none of those solutions really works. The mere fact that there are so many incongruent solutions (all these variations) reflects that counsellors have not been able to come up with reasonably dependable solutions.
394. We must realize that the present solutions and simpler books that focus on quick fixes cannot help people. It is like building a house without a foundation.
395. The matters of love and relationships in modern societies are more complex than the laws of physics, because they hardly submit to any logic or formula.
396. The worst kind of therapy is when couples are encouraged to play phony roles to express passion or compassion as a mechanism for saving their relationships. Role-playing is obviously an artificial activity that might induce more frustration in the end if partners are not intellectually (and emotionally) convinced about the authenticity of their own (or their partner's) feelings and words.
397. The fact that some people cannot express their feelings is often not due to a lack of communication skill. In most in-

stances, the problem lies deep in the psyches of individuals and it is often beyond repair.

398. It is time for a more comprehensive approach to study the nature of relationship problems. We must study the needs of our new society and scrutinize all the emerging facts.

399. We must study *what* has changed in society, *how* they are affecting relationships, and *why* radical changes are needed.

400. We must admit that our perception of reality (and life) is severely damaged nowadays as we have introduced more artificial needs in our lives and because we have been propagating a lot of shallow jargons about the meaning of life and happiness. Thus, our challenge is to develop relationship principles that fit the new reality of relationships.

401. The major assumption for couples must be that the likelihood of their relationship failing is much higher than succeeding.

402. Accordingly, couples must depend on some kind of guidelines and personal wisdom to make their relationships last.

403. Most importantly, we must plan and behave according to the statistics and experiences around us. They all indicate that *marriage is a temporary arrangement* unless a miracle makes it last as long as we hope it should.

404. On the other hand, this highlighted awareness might actually motivate us to extend realistic efforts and save our relationships. Our new approach to see relationships as a temporary arrangement can actually help couples make it last longer.

405. We must reconsider our view of relationships, redefine our expectations sensibly, and be prepared for the worst scenario, i.e., separation.

406. Why partners wait until they hate each other so much they cannot even look into each other's eyes? Why not separate civilly as soon as they realize they cannot relate to each other realistically. Why do not they remember that in most cases people cannot change?

407. Following our present approach would only make finding a companion more difficult due to i) couples' excessive expectations from relationships, ii) their rising mistrust, iii) the complexity and ambiguity of values in modern societies, and iv) occupational stress.
408. At the same time, the first sign of disagreement, nowadays, leads to partners' power struggles to establish their territories and inform each other of their urgent personal needs.
409. Partners' urge for assertiveness engages them in all kinds of destructive schemes, supposedly to make the relationship work. They play games and resort to retaliation even when their intentions might be unselfish.
410. They do so because they do not know of any better method to curb their frustration and deal with relationship conflicts that keep growing every day. They often play these games merely for the sake of forcing a solution. They sincerely feel they are helping their partner and their relationship.
411. However, usually these games and retaliations end in disaster. Even the most civilized games, such as a temporary withdrawal, could lead to a long-term confusion and an irreversible alienation process.
412. Often, a partner may simply behave somewhat passively until a solution for their relationship is found. Then the other partner reacts in a retaliatory way as well. For example, he/she does not feel or wish to have sex until the other partner responds to his/her ELove needs. Meanwhile, partners find each other's demands unrealistic. They find each other's retaliations a kind of blackmail. Therefore, the game heats up. A partner's decent objective for a temporary withdrawal—to signal his/her partner about the existence of a conflict between them—is not perceived or responded to in the same way his/her partner expects.
413. During this process, the mental or sexual deprivation puts added pressure on both partners. They take the threat to

their needs for compassion and sex seriously. They get hostile.

414. All along, the point ignored by both partners is that their partners might have had good intentions, at least initially. Both partners might have in fact been genuinely trying to salvage their relationship. Albeit they do not know how to make their points clear to one another.

415. All these conflicts and confusion are not necessarily a matter of bad communication either. Couples are living in such an imaginary world they do not even understand the nature of problems, even though they insist that they do.

416. More importantly, they ignore that often it is merely their own personal needs and expectations that require adjusting; and not their partners' attitude.

417. As stated before, most of our personal needs in new societies are artificial anyway. Our needs for more things and more compassion are what we have imposed upon ourselves by habit and imitation.

418. We have become too demanding because we believe we deserve better. We have become too ambitious and spoiled. Our phony social values have made us too needy and desperate.

419. Therefore, in most cases, merely our needs must be adjusted if we really were interested in the health of our relationships. We simply must learn to look at the bigger picture and stop fussing about our long list of artificial needs.

420. We must find ways of fulfilling our personal needs independently, so that the burden on relationships is reduced.

421. People are normally better in retaliation than finding a means of reconciliation. This is human nature. This habit shows humans' inherent limitations.

422. We are unwilling to accept that our spouses often cannot fulfil our personal needs merely due to their unique characteristics and not necessarily out of spite.

423. So, in the end, partners' honourable intentions get lost amidst their psychological deprivations and clashes. Soon, both partners face major catastrophes: Their personal needs are not satisfied, and they must face their partner's retaliations too. Things get out of control. Relationships fall apart.
424. We must then either submit to our partner's demands, which are normally outside our means and beliefs, or prepare ourselves for further struggles and alienation. In either case, we introduce more destructive games and retaliations into our relationships. Thus, the war of nerves continues until our relationships are out of control. This is an obvious scenario that we are all familiar with…
425. But is it natural? It can be counter-argued that relationship inconveniences are a reasonable price to pay for its advantages. Considering the benefits and the joy of relationships, we will continue to get ourselves into this difficult conundrum time and again regardless of all the warnings.
426. Especially for younger people with all kinds of hopes and urges, relationships will continue to appear a safe haven despite all the daunting evidences in society. They ignore the high likelihood of future agony for the sake of the immediate pleasure of someone's company *now*—another major repercussion of living in the now.
427. Nevertheless, we cannot avoid the temptation of getting into relationships, but we must become more conscious about its devastating pitfalls too. We must be better equipped to deal with its inevitable hardships, and know how to get out of it—which most likely becomes necessary—with the least amount of damage.
428. All along, each partner in a relationship feels the burden of unfulfilled personal needs, plus the added demands of his/her partner to make him/her happy.
429. Moreover, a 'relationship' creates a variety of needs of its own, as will be explained in Chapter Eight. Most often these needs remain unrecognized and unfulfilled, which

then cause added confusion for partners personally and in terms of relating to one another. The most obvious ones are created once children are brought into the equation.

430. Parents, already burdened by unfulfilled personal needs and their partners' demands, suddenly have to deal with the needs of the children too. Furthermore, they usually have conflicting strategies for satisfying their children's needs as well.

431. On top of all this, children's needs are getting too complex and irrational these days anyhow. We are allowing, actually encouraging, this to happen without proper justification. This is all part of social pressure to give children more love and things every day, and because partners like to satisfy their own Egos and their need for the love of their children.

432. The children's needs also limit partners' time and ability to attend to their own personal needs. Thus, they get edgy and blame their partners for all these inconveniences, at least subconsciously. A symptom of partners' deprivation (for compassion) emerges when parents begin to compete and fight for the love of their children.

433. Each parent tries to prove his/her love to the children by spoiling them more, and sometimes badmouthing or humiliating his/her partner. They do all these ridiculous crimes with the aim of satisfying their own personal need for compassion, which now they hope to satisfy partially through their children at least.

434. Therefore, in every relationship, three sets of unfulfilled needs (personal needs, their partners' demands, and relationship needs) place unmanageable pressures on both partners. And, then, these subdued needs and demands keep piling up and causing more tension, clashes, and retaliations.

435. The complexity of the relationship environment and our passivity about it are the reasons why it will take at least a century to find real solutions for relationships. However, we

can improve our relationships immediately by making some moderate changes in our personal mentality.

Chapter Seven
Relationship Perceptions

The discussions in the previous chapter show how we are misperceiving the purpose and capacity of relationships, the authenticity of our needs, and the meaning of life in general. Our perceptions are often erroneous because we are biased naturally due to our genetics and cognition, while influenced by social conditioning too. Accordingly, we misjudge our partners and the health of our relationships regularly. Thus, this chapter elaborates on the causes of our misperceptions and our role to acknowledge and remedy the obstacles they cause.

436. Our accurate view of corruption and duplicity in society cause cynicism about people's truthfulness and authenticity. At the same time, this personal wisdom and warranted defence mechanism leads to a large level of misperceptions for people, especially in their relationships.
437. On the other hand, a vast amount of misperceptions is caused by our idiosyncrasies or communication hurdles.
438. Accordingly, conflicts arise while relationships are viewed and measured according to partners' misperceptions of themselves, their partners, their personal needs, and relationship needs.

439. Overall, five main sources of misperceptions cause the vast levels of miscommunications and conflicts in relationships:
    - Equivocation
    - Misrepresentation
    - Transference
    - Apprehension
    - Identity

    These sources of relationship conundrums and the rather complex topic of perceptions are explained in the book, *The Nature of Love and Relationships* by this author. Those discussions reveal the enormity of couples' misperceptions and their consequences on their relationships.
440. Besides causing miscommunications and ruining relationships, our misperceptions create deep personal confusions about who we are, what we need, and what can really make us happy.
441. At the same time, the main point (and obstacle) is that we, including our partners, cannot overcome our misperceptions readily, due to our deep psychological constructs. Our firm inner forces, i.e., instincts, genetics, habits, and impulses, drive our dogmatic perceptions and decisions.
442. One major hurdle in relationships is that we cannot perceive our own personality accurately. And we have difficulty judging each other's personality too—mostly due to our misperceptions.
443. Meanwhile, we have become the most snobbish people on earth throughout the entire history of mankind due to our misperceptions of our capacities and needs.
444. We lose our identity when our perceptions of our personality and the world contradict reality largely. Meanwhile, the lack of personal identity causes more confusion and misperceptions. It makes the job of adapting to our environment difficult and frustrating. This vicious cycle continues until

we are totally out of touch with reality and our purpose of living.

445. The fact is that we never know who we are despite our lifelong struggle to establish our identity. The reason is that we perceive ourselves and our personalities according to the inner forces shaping our attitudes, our biased perceptions of the world, and according to the bogus social standards that we are trying hard to adopt or adapt to.

446. In relationships, the task of developing our identity faces even a tougher challenge. This is because being in a relationship imposes a new puzzling role for partners just for the sake of making the best of the situation. And also because partners like to influence each other.

447. Aside from its spiritual connotation, 'Who am I?', as a philosophical question, reflects the complexity of our personalities and perceptions. We have all realized the difficulty of answering this question.

448. However, the question, 'Who am I?', also reflects the existence of another dimension of us, the self, which is unknown to us. The self, we agree, is different from either our perceptions of ourselves or other people's perceptions of us.

449. We are responsible for misperceptions in relationships when we keep insisting that we know who we are instead of trying to learn more about ourselves through self-awareness. We are also guilty for letting our misperceptions cripple our understanding of our partners, our means of communicating, and our ability to solve our conflicts.

450. As intelligent humans, we could assume that understanding about our real needs and who we are is our main mission in life. However, we are not even used to self-analysis to understand the extent of our defects and faulty perceptions.

451. Not only we assume and insist that we know who we are, but also we insist that our partners are fully aware of who they are (mostly as we perceive them!).

452. Once we set our minds about 'who they are,' positively or negatively, it becomes close to impossible to accept any counter argument about the validity of our opinions and perceptions.
453. If only we learn that our partners cannot learn what we insist they should learn, we may be able to better manage our relationships and assess our options realistically.
454. We are completely self-centred not only in terms of thinking mostly about our needs, but also in terms of imposing all those needs on our relationships.
455. The drastic rise in relationship conflicts is due to couples' misperceptions about 'who they are and who they can be.' They just keep portraying a pompous identity to prove their strong individuality.
456. The level of consciousness is a vital psychological factor in communications. Many conscious, subconscious, and unconscious motives or impulses drive our communications.
457. Mind and body are only tools. They are used by this powerful entity called 'the Self' or 'Cognition' to run our affairs, partly consciously and partly unconsciously.
458. Cognition and consciousness are the locus of all human attributes, behaviour, and decisions.
459. Our weaknesses and strengths are stored at all levels of consciousness. They affect us and people around us positively or negatively depending on our awareness. Awareness is simply the level of our consciousness and cognition that we have learned to master.
460. The importance of self-awareness becomes evident when we consider its objective to dig into our subconscious and unconscious territories and gradually explore the causes of our deep-rooted behaviour.
461. The importance of self-awareness is also to assess our perceptions and refine our life outlook and mentality.
462. For one thing, awareness helps us notice our insecurities and fears, e.g., about the risks of independent thinking and

behaving, including rejection and loneliness. We are too attached to society to dare resist its values and demands.

463. Human nature is another important factor that causes deep misperceptions for people, while their social values and environment provoke inherent human wickedness, instead of controlling them through morality to some degree.

464. Most likely, the idea of human purity is only a fantasy. Humans, like most other creatures in nature, are probably supposed to be wild and offensive to protect themselves and their own species. Except that humans are often careless about their own kind, anyway, as they keep killing one another in millions as a routine human lifestyle—a justified habit. So far, we have only proven human impurity.

465. Our search for tranquility and purity has emerged from humans' struggle to escape constant suffering and stress.

466. In fact, we might have an easier task proving that humans become more arrogant and unreliable as time goes by.

467. These depressing conclusions about human nature further confirm the earlier points about human limitations to grasp the requirements of relationships and coping with them.

468. Still some level of active involvement with life is better than neglecting ourselves and losing the opportunity of being a more conscious and conscientious person.

469. Most of our thoughts and decisions are processed beyond our control (in the subconscious and unconscious). The first benefit of this knowledge is that we appreciate the difficulty of effective communication more clearly. We understand the obstacles that everybody faces in communicating and running their relationships. We also learn about the destructive force of our misperceptions.

470. Learning about the levels of consciousness can enhance our objectivity, to judge our own and other people's behaviour better. More importantly, a few people may also acquire a capacity to tap the enormous power of subconscious and unconscious—toward enlightenment.

471. The three personality aspects of an individual match the three levels of consciousness very nicely. This reflects the correlation of a person's level of consciousness with his/her personality and behaviour.
472. The Model aspect of personality mostly operates from within the conscious level of one's mind. It represents mostly our sense of adaptation, playfulness, and sociability.
473. The Ego aspect of personality represents our subconscious mind, which reflects our private and selfish traits and motives.
474. The Self aspect of personality represents mostly our unconscious urges, instincts, potentialities, and spirituality inclinations.
475. Miscommunications and misperceptions keep influencing one another and piling up dangerously in the early stages of relationships. Once these misperceptions are deposited in various levels of couples' consciousness, there is very little anybody can do to reverse the deteriorating state of their relationships.
476. Our communications, perceptions, and consciousness (including the three personality aspects) are highly interrelated impulses. Collectively, they instigate our reactions and behaviour in any circumstance.
477. Our misperceptions and Ego cripple us to see the right success factors for maintaining our relationships.
478. Logic and common sense do not help solve relationship conflicts, because everybody has his/her unique perception of logic and common sense. Nowadays, there seems to be as many varieties of logic and common sense in relationships as the people in them.
479. Couples are living in such an imaginary world (due to their misperceptions) they cannot even grasp the nature of their relationship problems, let alone finding solutions within that imaginary setting. Thus, only some guidelines can help relationships prosper within some kind of orderly atmosphere.

Chapter Eight
Relationship Needs

As social values and personal needs of couples change during the course of history, the meaning, purpose, and format of their relationships should be reassessed and redefined as well. The reason is that the personal needs of individuals dictate the kind of relationships they are willing to accept for their novel lifestyles. Obviously, the changes in lifestyle and personal needs in the last few decades have been enormous. Yet, we have not developed a reasonably compatible framework for our relationships, hence the hectic situation we are facing. The nature of relationships in the new era and emerging trends are outlined in Part II. Relationship choices are discussed in Part III.

Throughout this book, but mainly in this chapter, the concepts of relationship needs, models, and framework are discussed without getting into their details. Those discussions are rather extensive and beyond the objectives of this book. Here, the intention is to present only the highlights of relationships conundrums in the new era. However, interested readers are encouraged to read about relationship needs, models, and framework in other relationship books in these series or in *The Nature of Love and Relationships,* which are all prepared by this author.

480. We must learn to view 'relationships' as a unique entity, which has specific needs very different from the conflicting needs of two partners.
481. We can say that *a relationship is a collection of partners' actions and feelings.* However, a relationship must also be viewed as a *system or atmosphere for facilitating partners' cooperation to achieve certain goals.*
482. Presently, no uniform set of objectives is available in society to guide couples in their relationships; to tame their wild perceptions of relationships' potentials and purposes.
483. Without a framework, the state of relationships would deteriorate beyond control very soon.
484. Without guidelines, even compatible couples are subject to gross misperceptions and loose interpretations about their relationships. (Relationship framework and guidelines are explained in Chapter Thirteen.)
485. A major purpose of developing a framework is to discuss and eliminate some of the gross misperceptions about relationships.
486. The framework can help partners learn and follow some guidelines to 'relate' to each other. They should stop hoping that the task of *relating* can happen automatically or by a lifelong trial and error. The framework would help couples set their objectives and expectations from relationships more realistically.
487. Another objective of the relationship framework is to identify a handful relationship models that can fit the variety of individuals' personalities, while providing the general advantages of being in relationships.
488. Realistically, couples must evaluate their personal needs in comparison with the relationship needs objectively and then choose the relationship model that best fits their personalities.
489. Of course, every relationship has its unique characteristics and setting. And there should be some level of flexibility in

relationships to accommodate all personalities. However, only a handful relationship models can support partners to relate to each other effectively.

490. The stress caused by new lifestyles and couples' misperceptions are crippling a good majority of relationships and also threatening the foundation of our societies in general. The situation is only going to get worse if new solutions and a framework for relationships are not found soon.

491. The first step for developing a framework is to redefine relationships as an *independent* setting, and not a collection of partners' erratic whims.

492. People are paranoid about fairness nowadays. A 'relationship framework' can replace the need for couples' constant fight for 'equality.'

493. The main objectives of a relationship framework are to:
- Enforce teamwork.
- Bring objectivity back into relationships.
- Increase communication effectiveness.
- Reduce partners' expectations from relationships.
- Overhaul individuals' mentality and social mechanisms.

494. Knowing about teamwork and actually being committed to it as the only solution for relationships are two different things.

495. For the mere reason that individuality is becoming the most important requirement of relationships, creating new methods of teamwork is imperative more than ever.

496. New methods of teamwork might contain a variety of tools, including a simple agreement between partners about sharing responsibilities and finances of the household and sticking to the plan.

497. Another role of teamwork would be to maintain some kind of balance between partners' personal needs and the relationship needs.

498. Once partners learn to focus on teamwork, their obsession for *equality* becomes obsolete. Instead of depending on equality, or superiority, the success of relationships would be measured only by the smooth operation and outcome of teamwork.
499. Indeed, the strength of teamwork lies on its emphasis on partners' independence and objectivity.
500. In line with our personal obsession for more things and affection, we have reduced the capacity of our relationships to be objective.
501. Without relationship guidelines and principles, partners' communications have become too subjective, Ego driven, and destructive.
502. The logic dictates that the more we promote individuality and personal rights, the less we should expect from relationships. We should become more self-reliant to maintain our independence.
503. A major task for partners is to always remember that their personal needs and relationship needs are not the same or coincidental.
504. They must remember that most relationship problems and misperceptions emerge because couples perceive relationship needs as an extension of their personal needs.
505. Accordingly, a great deal of soul searching and mental adjustments is needed in order to adapt our relationships to the new social framework.
506. We need modern thinking and principles for relationships to match the modern life we are so eagerly embracing.
507. Especially, the hoopla around positive thinking in recent decades has had some disturbing consequences on our perception of life. For one thing, we have lost touch with the harsh reality of life and believe that we deserve to have all the best of everything including a flawless, loving relationship. We have all become too idealistic.

508. Therefore, all our lives, we look for an imaginary idol to accept as our companion, or we try to rebuild (change) our partners to fit that image. Especially, there is a trend out there to make men softer so that they can respond better to women's desires and perceptions of relationships.
509. Everybody is unique (and most likely damaged) due to his/her nature, needs, and perceptions. Therefore, people's expectation to find or create their ideal partners is just too naïve. It is amazing how partners expect each other to behave the same way they think and feel themselves, as if such transformation was feasible or even desirable.
510. The question partners should ask themselves is whether they can find the right formula—relationship model—to relate to each other effectively and live a quiet life without trying to change each other.
511. We seldom get an opportunity to learn about some of the finer means of thinking and living. Even when we do, we have extreme difficulty staying on a path of awareness when people around us are consumed with superficial needs and spread phony values.
512. Instead of looking for an ideal, imaginary relationship environment, maybe our new goal should be to make relationships only manageable and tolerable. This requires conscious efforts to lower our personal expectations and define new objectives for our relationships.
513. At two extremes, a relationship may be viewed as a spiritual connection between two individuals, or as some boring obligation between them to share life's hardships.
514. Accordingly, we may perceive relationships as a sacred experience in beauty and selflessness, or only a means of social adaptation and self-gratification. While the latter position appears closer to reality, the former reflects our instinctual search for perfection and spirituality.
515. In new societies, people's perceptions of relationships cover both of above two extremes and everything else between

these two realms. In particular, more people strive nowadays to find their soul mates, while at the same time they are unable to cope even with the basic needs of their relationships.

516. Under this circumstance, we have no clear picture of what relationships are supposed to be (or can actually be). In general, we try to bring some degree of both practicality and romance to our relationships.

517. However, we do not seem capable to capture the sense for the right balance between practicality and romance. For example, most people have realized that signing a prenuptial agreement is necessary as a practical measure, but doing so still appears businesslike and unromantic to them.

518. We often fail to use common sense when it is wise to be practical, and we do not know how to express our emotions when it can sweeten a relationship. Therefore, we have not been able to bring either practicality or romance into our relationships. The reason is that social changes have been too drastic and misleading in recent decades. They have tainted our personalities, our perceptions of the world, and our relationships.

519. We have become too spoiled, needy, and impatient. Meanwhile, our relentless search for a reliable companion, usually with negative experiences and outcomes, is causing confusion, mistrust, and depression.

520. The truth is that our *urgent* emotional *needs* (e.g., need for sex, ELove, and security) overpower our ability to think practically about the potential catastrophes of relationships. This is particularly true because our spirits is usually weakened by other harsh realities of modern lifestyles.

521. Tension is increasing in relationships not only due to people's higher emphasis on independence, but also their ongoing self-pity for not having an ideal partner in their lives.

522. Nowadays people have a high opinion of themselves (often unrealistically) and thus set a high standard for their ideal partner and their needs from relationships.
523. For one thing, people like to exaggerate their self-worth to themselves and others in order to prove their identity.
524. Nowadays, people struggle for independence (identity) too obsessively. Consequently, their tendency to play phony roles and be popular creates many inner conflicts for them, because the more they try to prove their fake identity, the more they lose their innate identity.
525. Every day, life is getting harder to adapt to, while the fast deterioration of relationships' environment is the most direct (and costly) effect of our inability to adapt socially in a natural way.
526. People seem obsessed with their search for a soul mate nowadays, as they consider it a necessity and a right.
527. However, having a companion feels like a lot of work these days, too, and often the cause of more stress.
528. The level and complexity of partners' expectations have kept increasing as society promotes phonier lifestyles.
529. Realistically, though, the level of expectations from relationships should be reduced to compensate for the increasing pressures that society is placing on the personal life of people already.
530. As normal human beings, we are unable to respond to our rotating needs for independence and dependence.
531. Even worse, we are unable to respond to the rotating demands of our partners for independence and dependence.
532. Therefore, we must adopt a relationship model to handle our inability to handle all these imbalances between partners' somewhat random, but persistent, needs for both independence and dependence.
533. The existing social fervour for independence indicates that, as a rule, couples should place their emphasis on a relationship model that best guarantees partners' independence.

534. The higher we climb up the 'relationship needs tree,' a higher sense of dependence and maturity is required from partners. Accordingly, couples' rising urge for independence means that they should stick to models in the lower levels of the relationship needs tree.
535. Advocating independence in relationships might appear inconsistent with the objective of 'enforcing teamwork.' However, there is no conflict here, as 'teamwork' must be viewed as an objective negotiation process between two independent partners, and not their dependency.
536. Often our 'psychological construct' dictates the urgency of our needs. Therefore, the 'need urgency' concept suggests that for many of us being at a certain level of 'personal needs tree' is so urgent and important we can ignore all other needs, even if we face starvation or death.
537. All of our personal needs demand our attention at some degree and time. However, the need for a companion seems to be an everlasting, urgent, and imposing need, more like a basic need.
538. When couples cannot create a good balance between their personal needs and the relationship needs, they feel tension. Thus, each partner must convince him/herself honestly about his/her real needs, instead of agreeing to be in a certain type of relationship (model) hastily.
539. Partners may leave some room for leniency in terms of the relationship model they are comfortable with, but not too much at the cost of going against their natural needs. When partners cannot reach a reasonable compromise about a suitable relationship model for them, the situation offers the best indication that they are not made to be in a relationship together.
540. Even though couples should have the option of choosing the best relationship model for their type of personality and needs, normally they should start from the simplest relationship model, which is the lowest in the relationship tree.

They could then try to climb up the tree according to their actual experiences in their relationship and by showing their aptitude and personality strengths.

541. The 'relationship needs tree' and five simple relationship models are presented in more detail in *the Nature of Love and Relationships*. Yet, those models can be expanded and explained in a working manual. Couples can use that manual to identify the relationship model that suits them. Instead of the five models suggested in that book, we could possibly come up with a tree that supports about a dozen relationship models.

542. The relationship framework and mechanisms proposed in this book (Part III) put the onus on partners to be extra vigilant about their relationships and choose the right relationship model for them at the outset. It is their own fault if they get themselves involved in faulty relationships or do not end them quickly and peacefully.

543. In this setting, partners must have a proactive and progressive mindset. Most importantly, partners must view their relationship as a temporary arrangement, unless they can prove their expertise and sincerity to work together.

544. Relationships can no longer be viewed as a whimsical set of activities and needs to merely fulfil our emotional deficiencies. Being in a relationship is a serious *business* and must be viewed as such by partners.

545. The factors for success in relationships are quite different nowadays and they would most likely keep changing in the future according to changes in social structure. Thus, our approach to relationships' format, needs, models, and success should reflect this reality.

PART II

The Trends

Chapter Nine
Fundamental Trends

Many fundamental changes and trends in society have affected relationships directly and deeply. The most prevalent social impact has transpired in terms of people's rising personal needs and their expectations from life and relationships. The modern society is satiated with progressive philosophies and slogans that have induced grave misperceptions about the purpose life and potential of relationships. Thus, for assessing the prospect of relationships, we must examine the social trends, their impacts on relationships, and then find radical mechanisms that best correspond with the new needs of individuals. These trends are discussed in this and the next two chapters. Then radical solutions are offered in Part III to address our erratic personal needs and review our choices for coping within modern relationships.

546. A fundamental, emerging trend is that we value our freedom and identity a lot nowadays. We are giving the highest level of emphasis to our personal need for independence more than ever in human history.

547. Many reasons exist for this development. The main reason is that women are finally given equal rights. Due to their ef-

forts, everybody is now more aware of their personal needs for independence and identity. This major premise, i.e., the need for independence, should then be our best guide in developing the new principles of relationships.

548. The second fundamental development is that nowadays people are constantly playing various roles and games to portray an appealing personality, mask their idiosyncrasies, adapt to social values and demands, and manipulate (control) others.

549. The contradiction between the above two prominent trends, i.e., people's drive for independence (identity) and their tendency to play phony roles to be popular, creates inner conflicts for them, because the more they try to prove their identity through superficial means, the phonier they become and the more they lose a chance to find their Self.

550. Accordingly, a majority of people are losing their touch with both life and their identities more every day, because of not only their overall misperceptions, but also the roles and games they are forced to play to stay popular and be accepted in society.

551. For one thing, we like to exaggerate our self-worth to ourselves and others in order to prove our identity and boost our popularity. Thus, we are not as authentic as we should be in our encounters. We have indeed become quite estranged with our true nature.

552. This debilitating condition has created all kinds of problems for us in terms of finding the right companion, communicating, and perceiving our partners. Meanwhile, we seem even less capable to define our identity without a reliable partner.

553. The situation gets worse when counsellors make couples play still another category of roles to solve their relationship conflicts. These new roles create even more confusion for people in terms of who they are and how they should be relating to their partners. People's habitual unauthentic roles and games are at least familiar to them and partially justi-

fied emotionally and intellectually. However, their new roles (suggested by counsellors) often cause more anxiety, as they contradict both partners' existing roles and true nature.

554. The third fundamental new trend in society is that couples place a much higher emphasis on their personal needs than relationship needs. In fact, they are hardly even aware that certain relationship needs exist, which must be satisfied way ahead of partners' needs.

555. Accordingly, partners naively expect their relationships to be functional (maybe even ideal, according to their subjective criteria), and also assist them in achieving their personal goals. If a relationship cannot fulfil these high expectations, they want out.

556. We are no longer willing to tolerate mediocre relationships. We are now more important than our relationships. Some readers may wonder whether this has not been the case before. No, our old values inherently placed the needs of relationships ahead of individuals, according to tradition and religion. However, we are now past those outmoded systems.

557. Now individuals wish to be more important than their relationships. We keep insisting that life is too short and we live only once. Therefore, we wish to take advantage of life as much as possible before it is too late.

558. In a nutshell, we can say that in the older times the emphasis was put on 'survival,' whereas nowadays the emphasis is placed on 'happiness.' (By the way, 'survival' is still the main objective of relationships in less modernized countries where people are facing pressing life dilemmas.)

559. Of course, our emphasis on happiness does not mean that we are happier people than past generations or those living in less spoiled countries. Rather, we just like to think (and pretend) we are happier. We want to show our resolve to find that elusive happiness. Why?

560. There are three major reasons for our incessant quest for happiness: **First,** we have been brainwashed to believe that happiness is out there and we can easily find it by satisfying our artificial needs for wealth, power, and love. Therefore, we keep struggling to satisfy these artificial needs with no end in sight or real happiness in our hearts. In fact, we are becoming more depressed every day, as we introduce more artificial needs in our lives, lose touch with reality, and then fail to feel the expected happiness thereupon. **Second,** we have been learning and propagating a lot of philosophy about life and happiness in recent decades. We like to talk a lot about happiness and prove our ability and conviction to build a happy life. All these exaggerated ideas about positive thinking, living in the now, and similar philosophies are screwing our ability to perceive reality. **Third,** the increasing depression and suffering in society make us more edgy and eager to find happiness, and we become more susceptible to all these philosophical gimmicks too.

561. As societies grow, we suffer more and thus seek relief (happiness) more obsessively. Actually, the above noted three reasons are interrelated. They have evolved to support (and also incite) one another: That is, we try to avoid (deny) reality by making up all kinds of philosophies in order to mitigate our suffering.

562. The above trends reflect our new mentality. And we cannot change it. Therefore, our challenge is to develop relationship principles that fit this new reality (perceptions).

563. Another fundamental trend is that the old premise to depend on partners' romantic vows to love and cherish each other forever regardless of health and wealth is no longer helping them. Our daily experiences confirm that it is not working anymore. So, let us be honest about these facts. Those good (or bad) old days are long gone.

564. Another major trend is that, in recent decades, old values and relationship guidelines have been eradicated without

new ones replacing them. We have only developed more unrealistic expectations for our relationships every year.
565. Moreover, we make subjective judgments about the health of our relationships merely based on our personal perceptions and needs.
566. To avoid these misleading approaches and reverse some of the troubling trends, we need a simple set of relationship guidelines that makes sense to everybody and fits our new social reality.

The noted fundamental trends and erratic changes in lifestyles have influenced people's mentality regarding their personal needs, which then affect their behaviour in their relationships. Therefore, many other trends are also noticeable in the new era:

567. Social complexities, phony values, egotism, sexuality, and personal needs are rising irrationally. Accordingly, relationships are becoming too complex and difficult to define and tolerate.
568. People's expectations from relationships have risen erratically, because they not only consider relationship needs merely an extension of their personal needs, but also see relationships a means of finding happiness.
569. Accordingly, people's stress level keeps rising every year due to relationship conflicts and unfulfilled expectations, while socioeconomic and career demands put a lot of pressure on them too.
570. Nowadays people find their relationships less bearable than what they had imagined them at the outset.
571. People's inner conflicts and agony keep increasing due to a sense of loneliness and insecurity, whether they have a partner or not.

572. All along, people's needs for both independence and dependence continue to rise. Accordingly, couples find less ground to relate and work as a team.
573. Meanwhile, the rate of relationship failures will continue to climb as people's personal needs and social complexity increase.
574. Each partner considers his/her individuality and independence the most important needs, in and outside of his/her relationship. They consider themselves too important and deserving to live a full and happy life. Thus, if relationships hinder these needs in some ways, they always choose their welfare above that of their partner and relationship as a whole. They want out if their relationships hinder their high aspirations even slightly.
575. Considering the above trends, couples' commitment to their partners and relationships is at best conditional. They stay in a relationship only if their partner can fulfil their personal needs and keep them happy.
576. People gauge the wellness of their relationships based on their selfish perceptions and misleading values, because no principles exist nowadays to guide the direction of their relationship or to judge its health.
577. People's current approach and attitude fuels the process of social deterioration, while they face more conflicts in relationships and become more impatient too.
578. The above trends are entangled in a vicious cycle that is spinning out of control. Thus, we should expect more of all the above facts in the years to come.

In line with the above fundamental trends, the basic nature of relationships is changing fast, too, and thus another set of clear trends are emerging, as listed below:

579. Nowadays, most people do not look for a partner to merely satisfy their basic companionship need. Rather, they want

their relationships make them happy, satisfy a host of their personal needs, and solve their personal problems. Accordingly, they blame their relationships for their personal failure to find peace and happiness.

580. Personal idiosyncrasies and insecurities have kept rising as social values have deteriorated, and vice versa. This vicious cycle would continue to spin out of control and make the success of relationships less likely every year.

581. Couples' insecurity and need for retaliation have reached such extremes that they kidnap, terrorize, or harm their own children just for intimidating their estranged spouses. The intensity of child custody and separation battles also shows how ineffective our relationship mechanisms are.

582. The possibility of finding our soul mate is getting slimmer every year. However, we keep struggling and stressing ourselves more, because of our sense of loneliness and desire to stay positive. Our romantic search for a soul mate is preventing us from perceiving relationships realistically.

583. For keeping an acceptable companion (let alone a soul mate) partners must have many common interests and compatibility, be good humans, and know how to work on their relationships continuously. However, human nature does not support these requirements. In fact, the trend shows that we are getting more arrogant and greedy every year and thus making ourselves less capable of getting along.

584. Considering the above trends and hundreds of other reasons explained in this book, marriage is becoming less stable and manageable every year. Thus, it seems more necessary to view marriages as a temporary arrangement, unless both partners gain all the high qualities required for building an effective relationship.

Chapter Ten
Social and Moral Trends

All the facts and trends noted in the previous nine chapters reflect the intensity of social and moral decline and its adverse effect on humans' morale and happiness. However, we have neither taken the time to understand the nature of new relationships, nor developed relationship guidelines and mechanism to accommodate the requirements of our new lifestyles. Accordingly, we can see the following social and moral trends:

585. We have now created a society satiated with all kinds of shallow ideals and slogans about our hectic relationships.
586. We depend on rudimentary rules, phony roles and games, marriage counselling, and laws to deal with the symptoms of relationship conflicts and breakdowns.
587. Even after we understand the roots of the problems and the need for new guidelines, we hardly get serious about developing a new mentality and a workable relationship mechanism.
588. It is easy, thus, to conclude that it would take us a long time to grasp the depth of relationship conundrums. It would take

us even longer to prepare and propagate a new framework that can help couples relate more effectively.

589. Proposing any kind of timeframe for reversing the deteriorating trends in relationships would be subjective. However, if someone really insisted to know the author's personal opinion, he would offer the following estimates and dates:

1) By the year 2115, couples and society will develop a good grasp of relationship hurdles and implement the needed radical changes.

2) By 2150, tangible progress in relationships will be witnessed globally, if more catastrophic events do not distract us altogether.

590. Suggesting the above, or any kind of, dates sounds ridiculous, even to the author himself, considering the dismal future of humanity in general if we follow our present path. The social challenges facing us in terms of water and food shortage, global warming effects, the rising sea levels, seemingly inevitable wars, and numerous other natural and manmade catastrophes might bring humanity to its knees in only a few decades anyway.

591. Our distraction by various socioeconomic issues is indeed another reason that relationship problems might not be dealt with in any speeder manner.

592. On the other hand, the scope of social catastrophes might automatically reduce our expectations from relationships immensely when we are forced to concentrate on the matter of survival, somewhat like the humans of the Stone Age. In that kind of environment, all the present fuss about relationships would be thrown out the window.

593. Nonetheless, we must plan according to our most optimistic assumptions about the future of humanity. We should put some relative faith in humans' resilience and eventual awakening to deal with the variety of problems we have created for ourselves and our relationships.

594. The criteria to gauge 'relationship related' progress consist of lower percentage of divorces, less dysfunctional and stressful families, a better balance between personal needs and the relationship needs, and longer lasting relationships.

Is Year 2115 a Good Target?

Considering the fast deteriorating situation of relationships and the rising personal stress due to socioeconomic conditions, the year 2115 is probably a reasonable ballpark to see an active change of attitude toward relationships. On the other hand, we can improve our relationships personally right away if we adopt a new mentality and act more realistically accordingly to the facts suggested in this book.

Some readers may find 2115 too pessimistic. They could argue that if real problems existed in relationships, people would tackle them quickly rather than wait more than a century to help themselves. Actually, they might suggest that the situation would auto-correct itself if a real need for change becomes evident. However, various discussions in this book show why our personal interests and flawed reasoning stand in our way of giving a higher priority to sanitizing our relationships. In particular, it seems plausible to anticipate the following trends:

595. The relationship situation is not going to auto-correct itself, as many conflicting forces overwhelm relationships nowadays, which disallow any kind of straightforward development of ideas. Rather, a direct, solid intervention is required to enhance everybody's awareness and willingness to study and improve relationships.
596. On the other hand, it would probably take us a long time to eventually see the need for a Generally Acceptable Relationship Principles (GARP) and other relationship mechanisms.

597. Even then, it will take a long time before GARP and other relationship ideas are adopted and functional. The reasons are obvious: People are nowadays too preoccupied with many complex, daily routines to take GARP seriously. They are not experts in finding solutions, and they have too rigid mindsets to accept radical changes. Few of us really appreciate the depth of relationship problems despite the overwhelming evidence before our eyes and the suffering we endure.
598. It appears that we have a great appetite for denial in order to sustain our hopes for finding love and happiness sooner or later. Our sad experiences with our love affairs are not teaching us much about the repercussions of our romanticism.
599. On top of this, social mechanisms are not progressive enough yet in line with social changes and couples' demand for independence and individuality. Social mechanisms, mostly legal systems, must be adapted to the new social realities, so that people can adjust their mindsets too.
600. Some magical forces might cause rapid improvement in the state of relationships. Some people or scholars might even believe that the existing situation would become tolerable with some minor modifications that couples can learn to incorporate in their relationships quickly. However, the author doubts these possibilities. Again, the chance for some kind of auto-correction looks dismal to the author. On the contrary, the need for some drastic intervention seems to be inevitable if we wish to suffer less.
601. On the other hand, some people and scholars may find the suggested dates of 2115 and 2150 too optimistic. They probably have many good arguments to support their claims. The author is rather inclined to agree with them. However, let us take a middle ground and hope that some kinds of solutions can be found by the next century. Nonetheless, choosing a certain date is not meant to be scientific

or essential, but rather a scheme to reflect the difficulty of the job at hand as far as the author can say.

602. In order to be a little bit more specific about the question 'Why 2115,' however, we should study the following topics:
- The *socioeconomic trends* regarding relationships, (presented in this chapter),
- The ***emerging relationship circumstances*** in the new era (presented in the next chapter), and
- A tentative timetable that seems reasonable for ***implementing radical remedies*** to bring some order to relationships (presented in Chapter Fourteen).

The following **Socioeconomic Trends** are observed in the new era:

603. Our economic systems, mainly consumerism, are forming our social values. People have gained a great appetite for objects and ideologies, hoping to buy more things and happiness by accumulating wealth.

604. 'Life is too short' and 'you live only once' have become the main mottos for most of us. Therefore, people jump out of their relationships to find a better partner and thus enjoy their presumed short lives the best they can. The basic requirements of relationships are ignored in the clouds of confusing slogans, misperceptions, and superficial values.

605. The increase in personal needs (for objects and compassion) has directly resulted in the decline of both moral and morale in society, while couples have raised their expectations from relationships enormously too.

606. The impact of higher expectations from relationships has been two folds: First, it has created additional personal stress that infects relationships. Second, we have come to believe that relationships can satisfy many of our emotional and financial needs. Couples assume that their partners are

psychologically capable of providing all the love they seek. They demand more attention and affection to soothe their personal hurts and the stress of living in our chaotic societies. Therefore, in effect, they are weakening the potency of their relationships.

607. Couples try to live beyond their means, at a higher standard of living than they can afford or deserve. This is an added source of pressure, while partners drive to find that elusive happiness at all cost. They demand more regardless of their means. Family debt per capita in relation to their income is at its highest level ever, due to crooked family values and consumerism. Family crises are getting out of hand due to the lack of partners' sensibility about budgeting and their finances.

608. New societies have advocated the concepts of equality and individualism. Partners' drive for independence and identity has turned relationships into a battleground for couples to establish their territory and superiority. Thus, the role of teamwork in relationships is not gaining the needed attention.

609. Couples abandon their relationships more often by the simplest signs of inconvenience. They want to give ourselves the highest chance of finding happiness in another relationship as soon as possible.

610. No longer any principles are available to guide couples, nor any standards exist to measure the health of their relationships. Therefore, couples depend on their own subjective viewpoints or the advice of friends and family to justify their crooked conclusions about the state of their relationships.

611. Couples consider 'love' the main factor for relationship success, not only for starting one, but also for sustaining it. The problem with this approach has been discussed in detail in Chapter Four and other parts of this book.

612. Relationships have become too complex to grasp and too demanding to cope with. Meanwhile, couples are not even trained about the basic relationship needs, the psychological effects of their encounters, and how deeply they are affected by their genes and rearing conditions. They forget that people's mindsets or personalities cannot be changed simply because their partners are expecting them to change.
613. The number of divorces and separations has skyrocketed in the last few decades without raising adequate alarm in society.
614. The amount of frustration and stress in the surviving relationships is increasing, too, due to partners' oversensitivity and unfulfilled expectations from relationships. Partners are also burdened by their indecision about staying in, or leaving, their dysfunctional relationships.
615. Stress levels in society and organizations have risen drastically due to the complexity of work and interactions, employment uncertainties, discriminations, international competition, and managers' obsession to serve themselves instead of attending to their social responsibility.
616. Accordingly, the level of stress in families has also increased because, nowadays, usually both partners work outside the house and are exposed to extreme pressures, especially women, who have been subject to more abuse and discrimination in organizations.
617. All the bad values and habits of organizations, such as hypocrisy, power struggle, and arrogance have infected relationships too. Partners follow the same rules to assert themselves at work and at home. Some women might actually perceive their husbands as abusive bosses in the work environment as well as at home.
618. Personal stress due to social demands and substandard relationships makes couples testy and impatient. They bug each other exactly at the time that life is confusing enough and

out of control already. Yet, they expect each other to be more romantic too and show their honesty and trust as well!

619. To remedy relationship problems and enhance communication, counsellors encourage role-playing and love expressions. Yet, relationship problems keep rising. This trend shows that the existing schemes, especially role-playing, are not working. Logically, relationship conflicts would only rise, unless partners are naturally convinced about the feelings or words they exchange. In fact, all these role-playings, as well as phony values, have made couples lose their identity and authenticity even faster in recent decades.

620. Companionship is probably the most important (basic) need of individuals nowadays and the one that is most often left unfulfilled. The importance of 'need for a companion' is evident in the wide range of personal needs it could potentially satisfy, as discussed in Chapter Two. Most people think and dream about a good companion as much as they think about food, consciously or subconsciously.

621. A crucial fact that couples ignore when they start their relationships is that, **nowadays the chances of relationships failing are higher than surviving.** The idea of finding a soul mate usually turns into a sour fate when they only end up in substandard relationships. Couples ignore this vital fact at the outset and do not do enough soul-searching and planning in advance.

622. Couples are not trained and prepared to handle the relationship needs, especially about the most likely scenario in their relationships, i.e., separation.

Chapter Eleven
Personality and Gender Trends

The socioeconomic trends noted in the last chapter, and all the facts discussed in this book, reflect the sad reality of relationships in the new era and the way these emerging trends are impacting everybody rather imprudently. Accordingly, this chapter provides another 160 emerging trends regarding the vast changes in peoples' personalities, which have then led to wider gender differences and conflicts. These trends reflect the emergence of many new complex dilemmas in relationship environment. They also show that reversing the deteriorating situation of relationships would be an uphill struggle and quite lengthy. **The references to 'people', 'men', 'women', or 'we' in the book, especially this chapter, do not mean everybody, but rather a significant portion of that particular category or gender.**

623. People seem to be living in a fantasy world with substantial needs and dreams. Their ambitions and needs for objects do not necessarily match their talents and efforts, and their needs for affection do not match their capacity to exchange compassion. Even when they are given wealth and compassion, they abuse it because they are not mentally prepared to

handle them responsibly. The more their selfish needs are satisfied, the more arrogant and greedier they become. Everybody believes he/she deserves more love and things.

624. Accordingly, the increasing amount of unfulfilled expectations from relationships has led to a great deal of frustration, retaliation, and hostility in families and society. Partners' oversensitivity due to untamed expectations has obscured even simple communications. For example, we hear often nowadays, especially from women, a phrase such as, "He/she does not know how to spoil me!" Many relationships break down every day because of this odd expectation. They do not even mind saying it so bluntly, as though 'spoiling' is a reasonable demand for relationships in the new era. Especially, after years of exploitation by men, now women want to be spoiled as if making up for the deprivations of past generations. They seek ELove, attention, and often obedience too.

625. At the same time, couples' rising sexuality, superficial needs, and unrealistic expectations from relationships have placed too much pressure on the social structure to provide general services and maintain a healthy environment.

626. The level of misperceptions and miscommunications in relationships are also increasing very fast and creating more havoc, as explained in Chapter Seven.

627. For one thing, couples have lost their sense of objectivity about the purposes and potentials of relationships, because they have become too idealistic and emotional about their expectations from relationships.

628. As a result, couples continue to jump out of their relationships faster and faster because they believe they can find another partner to fulfil their expectations better and give them the love and attention they deserve.

629. Thus, most of us struggle all our lives in search of an ideal relationship. Only a few of us might eventually realize our naivety after repeated failures.

630. Both single and married people envy each other's position and lifestyle. Everybody wishes to have the advantages of both lifestyles.
631. Married people do not appreciate the basic merits of their relationships because of their misperceptions about a single (independent) life and the possibility of finding love and happiness with a more suitable mate.
632. And unmarried people look for an ideal partner obsessively to fill the gap in their lives, while they brag about their freedom as a single person.
633. Besides our pleasure seeking mentality in the new era, our erratic urges for both dependence and independence are obviously playing a role in creating vast misperceptions about relationships too.
634. A disturbing feature of relationships in the new era is partners' rising appetite to play games in order to manipulate each other. The nature and extent of these games are becoming too complex and exhausting, thus making partners even more jittery and incompatible for building a sensible relationship together.
635. A main motive for these games is partners' need for personal expression or retaliation. They are the newly developed defence mechanisms that couples adopt in order to supposedly protect themselves.
636. Couples play these games and roles to maintain the balance of power in their relationships. This is an ongoing, onerous process, because partners simply seem incapable of putting down their guards, to live and relate naturally.
637. We play games and roles most of our lives to: 1) impress (charm), 2) flatter, 3) intimidate, or 4) snub someone. Therefore, the amount of time we are natural and sincere is minimal.
638. Hence, we are forced to play games and roles all our lives. We are somehow dragged into situations beyond our control where we must play along with others and assert our-

selves. Hardly anybody is natural these days. This condition is infecting relationships, too, as partners constantly feel obliged to play games and roles—out of necessity unfortunately.

639. Another dilemma is that even when a partner decides to stop playing games and behave naturally, he/she still cannot deal with his/her partner who is addicted to these relationship games.

640. The irony is that people always notice and criticize other people's games and phoniness, but ignore their own. Most often, they are subconsciously aware of the games and roles they are playing, but naively assume that people do not notice them. They believe in their playacting too much. Or even worse, they think people are too simple or busy to see through them.

641. People play roles and games also for maximizing their relationships' chances for success. However, by doing so, they actually increase the chances of being discredited and rejected.

642. A frustrating situation in relationships develops when a partner insists on playing a role or game and the other partner is not falling for it.

643. Relationships fail because too many of partners' games keep clashing. The more games they play to cope with social and relationship issues, the more conflicts arise, which then lead to even more games.

644. Usually one partner starts a game with a special intention. Then the other partner starts his/her own game instead of playing along. The first partner is astonished that his/her game is detected and resisted. They keep introducing more games until they are exhausted and angry.

645. People consider charming and manipulating others their absolute right and an effective tool, while they believe they are good at it too. So when they fail, they get upset and nasty

about it. All that charm turns suddenly into hostility and ruins even their basic friendships or means of relating.

646. The way people snub each other as a way of relating—to set the tone of their relationships and boost their Egos—is funny.

647. While need for control is common in humans, it becomes even more prevalent and damaging in relationships.

648. We try to control our partners in order to minimize the possibility of getting hurt by them, but also because we believe this would be the best way to protect our relationships.

649. As a result of all these games and phony roles, nowadays, too many people are always struggling to either find a companion or get rid of him/her.

650. Therefore, instead of expecting happiness from relationships, couples should actually be willing to pay a big price for it. This is a major fact they must accept before entering a relationship. Always a high price must be paid for the few fringe benefits of relationships.

651. We must be prepared to absorb the inevitable disappointments in relationships without resorting to retaliation and useless quarrels.

652. We must realize that anyone who is capable of retaliating harshly is inherently empty of compassion. In particular, it is quite silly when someone retaliates in order to force compassion in their relationships.

653. Love and anger are not compatible. Whoever uses anger to force (or keep) love is simply incapable of giving or receiving love.

654. With the advent of various dating facilities, people meet and learn about many candidates for dating. While this flexibility seems helpful to find a match, it also increases people's false hopes about the possibility of finding a qualified person soon. Therefore, they become too fussy and keep joggling a bunch of relationships. Meanwhile, people who are

truly suitable for being in relationships are becoming scarcer too.

655. People keep multiple relationships because they are doubtful about the viability of any of them. In addition, it is more efficient to study a few prospect partners simultaneously, as it usually takes many years to get to know someone even slightly. Having multiple relationships can also help a person rebound faster if one of his/her favourite relationships fails. He/she has other relationships to lean on at least temporarily. All these justifications sound reasonable, but what a world we have created.

656. Our hopes to eventually find a soul mate is a naive incentive that stops us from making genuine efforts and commitments in a relationship or keeping our promises.

657. Under these tough circumstances, perhaps the best definition for a soul mate is, 'Someone we can get along with, finally!'

658. Another cause of the increasing mistrust in society and relationships is that everybody is aware of the games people play, including multiple dating. Therefore, it is hard for people to take their relationships seriously.

659. Oddly, however, everybody is also too eager and hopeful to find a reliable companion as if s/he would arrive from another planet. People's struggle and optimism to find love, trust, and happiness are both admirable and depressing. It is depressing because people seem to miss, or eager to ignore, the new realities of relationships.

660. Instead, people's reaction to the present relationship conditions is just to do more of the same, i.e., more games, multiple dating, lying and mistrust, more shallow relationships. Thus, the rising frustration and stress in society. Ironically, they still hope to succeed in finding a reliable companion and living happily ever after too!

661. We have become a special (spoiled) generation—asking for more love while getting more arrogant at the same time. We

do not realize that with more arrogance, we keep losing our capacity to give and receive love.

662. Our children are getting even more spoiled in terms of idealism and not appreciating the hardships of life. Therefore, the deteriorating trends in relationships would go downhill constantly for new generations.

663. Couples are losing more sense about the true success factors for relationships every day. Thus, they continue to insist on love and objects as the main requirements.

664. Couples judge the health of their relationships arbitrarily or based on phony values, because no authentic yardsticks exist for setting practical standards and measuring the success of relationships.

665. Couples have little patience and interest to learn about the basic problems of relationships in a serious manner, e.g., reading books like this one. At best, people have only time and patience for learning about some possible quick fixes, which have no ultimate value anyway. People read those kinds of books or follow a few of counsellors' advices only to show that they did something to improve their relationships and still it did not work.

666. All along, personal failures in relationships, ongoing clashes, and sad statistics keep increasing mistrust among partners. Yet, people still ask for more love to justify their relationships, define their lives, and find happiness. The big contrast is obvious when people insist on love while the overall trust is fading fast in society. Love in the absence of trust! How could couples really be sincere about their love expressions when deep down, in their subconscious, their sense of mistrust about people, including their partners, linger?

667. It is hard to believe that 'trust' can be rebuilt into relationships as a general social norm in the near future and couples become truly convinced about it.

668. Therefore, while couples pretend to start their relationships based on trust, deep down they remain justifiably sceptical about it. This is true despite their convincing expressions of love and the roles they play mostly through MLove.
669. Satisfying our sexual urge is a practical choice in a modern society, but confusing it with love is hypocritical and impractical. The meanings of love, lust, and trust have become too intermingled and convoluted. This is causing additional mistrust and shakier social values. All those sleeping around with different partners and then talking about finding love are not congruent values or plans.
670. Overall, it is naïve to depend on 'love' or 'trust' to build a relationship. Instead, couples need objective mechanisms and a relationship framework to map their joint life.
671. Couples are unaware of their personal flaws and also how badly everybody gets damaged psychologically during their relationship experiences. They believe that not only they are flawless, but also enough perfect people are out there to choose for companionship. Therefore, they keep searching for some untenable ideal life that matches their fantasies.
672. In the older times, couples used to believe that marriage's most important objective was to share the hardships of life together. They knew how difficult life really is. They were ready and willing to make personal sacrifices and help each other sincerely. They played their angelic roles to reduce each other's burdens.
673. However, nowadays many couples do just the opposite. For one thing, people are pushing themselves to stay positive and believe that life is splendid and manageable. Therefore, instead of sharing life's hardships, they demand happiness and create more burdens for each other with a slight sign of inconvenience. Their unrealistic expectations and dreams about marital life make them view any nuisance an unacceptable barrier in their relationships. And they want to abandon their partners rather quickly for the greener pas-

tures. Today's marital objectives are mainly revolving around partners' fixation for love, sexuality, and happiness.
674. There is a race in society to behave pompously, strive for a lot of things and compassion, and be highly competitive. Everybody also likes to be highly sociable, pretentious, and popular. When people go to work on Mondays, they keep asking one another what they did on the weekend as if gauging a person's worth and completeness.
675. Humans' inner conflicts are responsible for their confusion, stress, and suffering in life, which eventually affect their relationships too.
676. At the same time, humans' *elementary* inner forces to be good are always in conflict with the external forces goading them to be bad. The modern society advocates greed, hypocrisy, dominance, and arrogance just to name a few of the crooked trends in the new era.
677. People have become too opportunistic (users) and calculating, due to their negative experiences and conditioning, including their conviction that life is too short and precious. They use various schemes to strengthen their positions and get ahead, and they associate mostly with people whom they find useful to them in some ways. This general perception (about people's hypocrisy, calculating nature, and insincerity) affects relationships, too, because partners judge each other based on their shallow criteria of life, but also their overall mistrust.
678. How can people romanticism be sincere when most of them try to be practical too (often by being so calculating and materialistic) in such a chaotic environment? These are contradictory objectives. Our social setting is ruining people's perceptions of one another and 'love'.
679. Couples are less capable nowadays to perceive and judge their relationships in its totality. They are easily influenced by their own need urgencies, and they are easily irritated by single events. The overall advantages of relationships are

largely ignored due to fast egotistical judgments based on emotional episodes and erroneous perceptions.

680. The depth of relationship dilemmas noted in this book is horrendous already. However, the matter gets many folds more complicated because of the erratic ways that men and women perceive and deal with these relationship facts and dilemmas in the new era. Some of these emerging trends due to gender differences are discussed in the remainder of this chapter.

681. A 'typical woman' image is developing in the new era mostly due to women's recent efforts to achieve equality, individualism, and independence. They have created and portrayed a special role and identity for themselves. On the other hand, men have not yet tried to create and propagate an identity for themselves. They have not been active in projecting a picture of a typical man.

682. Yet, men are stereotyped as selfish and unromantic. In reality, however, men are simply lost and without identity, nowadays, because they have difficulty understanding and coping with women's new demands. They have difficulty defining and asserting themselves at this time, which then leads to withdrawal or aggression.

683. Men and women are inherently incompatible in terms of nature. Therefore, partners' effort to find their compatible companion is mostly a shot in the dark already. In addition, the new relationship approaches and games make the job of finding our soul mate many folds tougher.

684. Peculiar demands that men and women put on one another and the impressions they make on one another by their attitudes and games are causing more distance between them. These games are too difficult to understand or respond to.

685. For example, the marital conflicts caused by less trust and more demand for love are felt deeper by men. This is because men supposedly have higher logical tendencies than women who are more emotional. With their lower MLove

and Model, men are already handicapped in expressing love, but when trust is gone, the matter of expressing love becomes even more awkward for them.

686. On the other hand, women are more capable of expressing love, even when their trust is not high. This is due to their higher MLove and Model, of course. Men lack this flexibility but women have a hard time accepting this fact and instead wonder why men are so passive most often and not responding to their demand for attention as much as they like.

687. Unfortunately, the level of trust in relationships, and about our partners' words, would keep declining in line with the upward trend in relationship failures. Thus, expressing love with honesty would become even more difficult, especially for men.

688. Accordingly, men usually give up the possibility of finding a soul mate sooner than women do. They continue to look for a companion nonetheless, but not with the aim of finding love. Women continue to remain more romantic and optimistic about finding a soul mate due to their higher intuitiveness and Model.

689. Women have been able to bond and support one another to set the rules of relationships. They are creating a new culture that might eventually prove quite dysfunctional for maintaining relationships.

690. An advantage of women's bonding is that they get plenty of support when they leave their relationships. On the other hand, because of this bonding, and in line with the women's general attempt to propagate the new culture, they encourage one another to be least tolerant of their relationship flaws and abandon their spouses quickly.

691. Therefore, while women seem to help each other in terms of support after separation, they might also be sabotaging one another and causing more separations, *maybe even inten-*

tionally, by provoking one another with their progressive ideas and attitude.

692. Men, on the other hand, do not have a sense of empathy, nor enough Model, to soothe each other's hurts once they leave their wives. Part of this deficiency is because men keep their emotions private to protect their pride. Women show their emotions but move on faster.

693. Women are emotionally stronger by nature, and also due to their higher social adaptability and Model. This helps them in terms of rebounding quickly after separation. And then their ability to support one another helps them recover even faster and better. However, the same need for social adaptability and Model makes them quite anxious to find a new companion.

694. Women's intuitiveness, higher Model, and bonding ability give them more resilience and optimism about life and love, which help them adapt better to changes and disappointments. Overall, they do not get too discouraged by their failures in past relationships. Yet, the number of women on anti-depressants is twice that of men.

695. Conversely, it usually takes longer for men to heal their wounds and recommit themselves to another relationship, due to their lesser resilience and the lack of support after separation. This additional agony teaches them better lessons. Therefore, they usually delay getting into serious relationships.

696. Men's logic and mistrust usually override their emotional needs, unlike women. Yet, their lower social adaptability makes them more vulnerable in terms of submitting to women's whims out of loneliness—but not necessarily out of love.

697. Pessimism about finding a soul mate, or even a reliable companion, has made men passive and this is making women frustrated, and more assertive.

698. Women do not seek men necessarily out of love, loneliness, or merely for the sake of having a companion. They already have many companions in other women. Satisfying their social and security needs often takes precedence over their craving for love or even companionship. This is true despite the emphasis made about women's drive for love in the earlier notes. Women's higher urge for social adaptation make them seek a partner to fit and feel better in social gatherings, to complete their identity, and for support.
699. At the same time, ironically, most women believe in the likelihood of finding love and an ideal partner, compared with men who give up faster and thus seek a companion mostly out of loneliness and for satisfying their basic needs.
700. In fact, women appear to have a higher need and talent for all three levels of love, i.e., ELove, MLove, and SLove than men. This aptitude pushes them to pursue love at any cost, but also get depressed for failing.
701. Therefore, for women, both their higher social tendencies and neediness for love make them not only to believe in the possibility of finding a soul mate, but also more eager to pursue this objective.
702. Conversely, men prefer some seclusion. Thus, their need for a companion is more for avoiding total loneliness. Men like socializing too, of course, but it is not their main motivation for finding a companion. Men socialize mostly to make their mates happy, to be perceived as a sociable person, or to create variety in their lives.
703. Despite the women's urge for a companion, and their obsession to enjoy life at its fullest, the welfare of their children often gets a higher priority. Many women postpone their serious relationships with another man, after a marriage breakdown, until they feel their children's relative independence or readiness. Therefore, considering the sacrifice most women make for their children, they believe they de-

serve their children's higher love, which they usually receive more than fathers do.
704. Of course, many exceptions exist when women in particular go to all extremes to protect or acquire a new partner, even at the cost of hurting their children.
705. Fathers' traditional respect has diminished in families for several reasons. **First,** women have assumed the ultimate role and responsibility for raising children and they perform this difficult task with absolute authority and decisiveness. Children find their mothers in charge and their fathers passive with much less authority around the family. **Second,** mothers dedicate themselves to their kids more often than men do. Accordingly, children in turn take a keen note of their mothers' devotion. Children feel a higher bond with their mothers instinctually, too, the same way mothers feel toward their children. **Third,** children see their mothers more vulnerable and needy for attention, especially because women can show their vulnerability through Model cleverly. So children feel obliged to take care of their mothers more than they see a need to sympathize with their fathers.
706. The bottom line is that men feel less involved with children and not receiving adequate love and respect. Their wives actually treat them a lot like another one of the children, including the use of an authoritative tone in their conversations with their husbands.
707. Nonetheless, the lower level of respect and power for fathers has made a negative impact on the wellbeing of the whole family.
708. The overall trend is that women are striving to create and express their new strong identity after many decades of oppression by men. They have learned to be assertive and support one another to establish their individuality and identity. Conversely, men are losing theirs due to the ambiguity of the gender roles and new relationship expectations. This is an accurate picture overall, yet the final outcome is ques-

tionable. For one thing, women's success to enforce their identity depends a lot on men's reaction to their demands and the roles that women expect of them to play. More importantly, however, both men and women can truly attain, and feel comfortable with, their identities only if they have a companion. Our everlasting, inherent urge to find our soul mates is the best indication of our sense of incompleteness (lack of full identity) without a good companion. Discussions in this book demonstrate that our need for a companion is an urgent and important need. It can potentially satisfy a large number of personal needs of humans stretching from the basic need for sex to the spiritual need for SLove. When these needs are not satisfied, few humans might attain enough psychological independency to affirm their identity in the new era.

709. Women may pretend that they understand, and are happy with, their emerging identity. However, when they reflect on their lives, they notice that their identity is incomplete and hurtful without a companion. Indeed, they need a man in their lives more than ever nowadays; more than men need a woman. This is due to women's higher Model and eagerness for social activity.

710. Therefore, women's identity is questionable without a man or while they are not happy with their companion. For one thing, they would be too preoccupied with the task of finding their soul mate, due to their optimism about finding an ideal partner. As stated before, men are not so optimistic about finding a soul mate, and they are less obsessed about having a companion (or even an identity) due to their lower Model.

711. Accordingly, if women's drive for identity reduces their chances of finding or keeping *competent* men in their lives, they would never find their true identity. 'Competent' refers to men who supposedly have a strong character (identity). No woman would enjoy a man with a weak character. A

man without a strong identity is worthless even for women. Yet, many women do not mind weakening their husbands' spirits.

712. A cynical observation about relationships in the new era is that sometimes women seek men mostly to exert their power over them; to prove their identity and superiority. However, this strategy fails for the reasons noted above.

713. It is absurd that all these conflicting forces are somehow corrupting relationship environments. Men are confused and lost for the time being anyway. However, their innate resistance and passivity are indeed damaging women's attempt to assert their own identity. This is especially true when the outcome is women's lesser access to *competent* men to support them mentally and physically.

714. Having emphasized on the fact that both genders need a companion to find their full identity, a more distressing fact must be stressed again as well. That is, even when they are in a relationship, neither gender can find their identities because of all their clashes.

715. Thus, genders' attempts to find their identities fail whether they are in a relationship or not, unless they adopt a more practical relationship framework to relate more effectively. The reason is that as long as the conditions for creating their identities are not pure and unselfish, partners continue to fight in order to enforce their perceptions of ideal identities for their genders.

716. In another word, partners' misperceptions of themselves and their partners, as well as their erroneous impression of ideal identities for their genders, prevent them from finding their true and practical identities. Besides, their continuous clashes suck the energy out of them to find and exert any kind of identity.

717. With no set identities, a large variety of inner conflicts overwhelms both genders. Thus, when couples meet, they want to set the tone of their relationships by playing all

kinds of games, all in hopes of manipulating and controlling their relationship at the end.

718. Two types of role-playing are introduced in relationships, both with adverse effects, while widening gender differences and quarrels too. First, the role-playing schemes that marriage counsellors advocate in order to stir up communication and love in relationships. The weakness of this technique is that as long as the real problems of a relationship are not understood by partners, playing roles only frustrates them. They must somehow grasp and tackle the main sources of their problems directly. All the superficial communications actually confuse them more and drive them away from the reality of their relationship.

The second type of role-playing has even a harsher impact on relationships. It begins from the minute partners meet and it continues throughout their relationship. They play all kinds of roles and games to impress, entice, manipulate, or deceive each other. They exaggerate in all respects in order to succeed: by flattering, getting too emotional, showing indifference, proving their independence and power, retaliating, and so many other games that go on throughout the process of dating and in their relationship too.

719. Couples like to play certain roles in order to set precedence and enforce their needs. They strive to set artificial boundaries to establish their superiority from the beginning. So, it is becoming impossible to sense sincerity and the true personality of people nowadays. This role-playing (including retaliations or reactions as defence mechanisms) might be somewhat justified considering that everybody gets hurt in relationships at some point. Couples play games to prevent more headaches. But then, they lose the chance of relaxing, being natural, and building an effective relationship.

720. By playing games, couples have also minimized their own level of objectivity as well as their partners'. Therefore, they

suffer personally while their relationships follow a destructive course too. By role-playing, couples are also losing the opportunity of finding companions who appreciate them for who they really are. Instead, they only struggle with their own phony personalities (to appear convincing and natural), as well as with their partners' (to understand them perhaps).

721. Nowadays, most people like to depend on their clever Model to play appealing roles for attracting love and sympathy. At the same time, they also try to hide their strong Ego and haughtiness behind Model. In a society where arrogance has found such a strong value, even Model often advocates pomposity. So, it is becoming difficult to understand who a person really is.

722. Women are becoming more active socially and placing a high value on living life to its fullest. They need to do more things, go to various functions, and travel extensively, all in hopes of finding that elusive happiness. At the same time, men are becoming more passive, content, and couch potatoes.

723. Overall, it is fair to say that women are the stronger gender in general. Men are a weaker gender, in terms of emotional vulnerability (personality), despite the fact that women are more emotional. The reasons for this seeming contradiction are explained throughout this chapter. Actually, men's weakness is widely known and propagated regularly in the new era. Even advertising agencies exploit this perception whenever they can benefit from it (see note 741 below). Women are also aware of the men's vulnerability. Therefore, it is natural that they might attempt to use this information to push their ideologies and obtain everything they believe they deserve.

724. Due to their higher reliance on intuition, decisiveness, and the teachings of the new culture, women are trying to be in charge of the family. They seem to be good at it, too, in many respects. However, in the process, they also feel the

need to prove their superiority to men. Well, since women are the stronger gender in reality, why should not they be in charge or try to show off their superiority occasionally? The problem is that any type of superiority by either gender cannot work in the new era where the emphasis must be placed on equity, individualism, independence, and satisfying personal needs and ambitions.

725. Therefore, when women try to prove their superiority, it leads to further deterioration of relationships and more mistrust. Except, of course, in the cases where husbands really prefer to be quite passive and/or submissive. Many women actually do not mind turning their husbands into submissive men in order to feed their own Ego and ELove. Some women might think, "Why not give it a try anyway and see if it works." However, in the end, this situation cannot prevail in progressive societies.

726. Relationships would go through a lengthy, unpredictable transition period while women try to assert themselves and find their identity. It would be a lengthy and frustrating process because their present approach is both impractical and illogical.

727. During this transitional period, women have difficulty being a modest (content) wife in an environment that advocates a domineering attitude to enforce equality and identity. Many women have been successful in practicing this approach in their relationships already. They present very appealing role models for the rest of them. Women's influence over one another is too strong to be ignored, by either women or men. Mothers, daughters, female colleagues and friends are all placing a lot of pressure on one another nowadays to behave assertively. Any woman who attempts to behave differently might be ousted. However, more importantly, she would feel miserable for not being a typical (assertive) woman like others.

728. It is quite likely that many men have become passive and submissive, because they have less capability for bonding together and are thus becoming weaker. Furthermore, they are less eager to develop and maintain a strong identity for themselves. Their logical minds, passivity, and neediness for a companion are keeping them the weaker gender they have probably always been.

729. Men's resort to violence and physical domination are indeed good clues about their inability to keep up with the kind of games that women are better at playing so naturally. Men's frustration is also due to their inability to keep up with women's needs, which men often find illogical often anyway.

730. Women seem to be winning most of the battles in relationships, but it is doubtful that any gender can win the war that is going on. The point is that, as long as one gender or one partner is weaker than the other, their relationship remains dysfunctional. There would not be enough respect and challenge for the stronger partner to stay in the relationship or take it serious enough. This fact is indeed most relevant in our new culture where individualism and self-esteem have found such a high value.

731. Therefore, women's urge to establish their superiority in the new era would not benefit anybody in the end. Women are behaving naturally, of course, according to their inherent personality strengths and strong bonding capability. Nonetheless, their effort is already putting relationships in great jeopardy. They would be the ones suffering the most from the repercussions of the existing situation, because they are more sensitive and they believe in love.

732. Obviously, relationships get into trouble because both partners are at fault in some respects. And also because the whole society is losing control over both the economy and relationship norms. Even when a partner is smart, patient, and humble to make the relationship work, the chances of

saving his/her relationship are still low. The reason is that his/her modest behaviour is perceived as a sign of weakness instead of goodness. He/she is treated poorly or ignored. Therefore, both partners are normally forced to be assertive, which usually turns into aggressiveness and quarrels.

733. The situation with relationships resembles the global warming mayhem. Nobody is willing to accept the existence of a fundamental problem or do anything about it. The main reason, also like global warming, is the economy. Materialism and hypocrisy would not allow partners to become more realistic about their approaches and social values they have adopted rather naively.

734. Women go into their next relationships with even more expectations instead of less. They believe that their reasons for leaving their past relationships (e.g., need for more love or compassion) had been justified and thus their new relationships must make up for everything they had missed before. They want to prove to themselves and others that they made a right decision to leave their previous relationships. Therefore, they look for more love, luxury, and security.

735. Conversely, men usually prepare themselves for less authority and set lower expectations if they decide to get into another serious relationship.

736. An effect of women's intuitiveness is that their priorities somewhat change quickly after having their children. For one thing, they are forced to exercise a lot of authority to make their children follow their rules. A mother is driven instinctually to manage her life as well as her children's. Therefore, she becomes authoritative, commanding, and demanding. These are mostly instinctual traits that surface when her life begins to get hectic with children, and maybe a lazy husband, testing her patience. She also finds less time for her husband after children are born. He is suddenly given a lower priority and importance, maybe not intentionally but rather practically. Furthermore, she learns eventu-

ally that it is more efficient and natural to treat her husband like another one of her children. Decisively, she has to get things organized and done quickly the way she has found productive through her child-rearing experiences. She finds these tactics, i.e., commanding, demanding, and impatience, most natural and effective for running the family affair.

737. For men, however, their wives' gradual (but drastic) change feels unnatural and annoying eventually. They attribute it to their wives' loss of interest and romance. In this environment, women look rather insensitive, impatient, and sometimes even cruel, in the way they run the whole household, including their husbands, so rigidly.

738. Overall, women play a more active role in shaping the relationship atmosphere and imposing the rules due to their decisiveness.

739. Men, on the other hand, are lazy to argue or fuss too much. Therefore, more women are becoming in charge of the family while men are becoming more submissive.

740. Accordingly, most partners, especially men, learn to stay somewhat passive in order to cope with their substandard relationship situation.

741. The existing culture hinders teamwork. Actually, an image of men's submissiveness (and maybe their idiocy) is propagated regularly even in TV commercials to sell products to women. For example, while writing this chapter, a couple of TV commercials caught the author's eyes. They reflect how social trends regarding relationships are grasped and exploited even by advertisers:

The first commercial was about Multigrain Cheerios. The box apparently refers to 120 calories per serving. The husband makes an innocent comment to his wife: "Are you trying to watch your diet?"

"Do I look like I need to watch my diet?" the wife asks with irritation and sarcasm.

"No, honey, I'm just stating what the box says (about its low calories)," the poor husband replies with a guilty tone in absolute panic.

"What else the box says?" the wife demands.

"The box says, 'Shut up, Steve.'" the husband replies with shame and misery. The wife smirks.

The second commercial was about McCain's Deep and Delicious frozen cake. The wife is enjoying the cake. And the husband is trying to draw his wife's attention and support about his dream of becoming a mime. However, she is not paying attention to his comments and enactment of some miming gestures, because she is absorbed by the taste of the cake. When she notices him finally, she demands with impatience, "What're you doing?"

The husband freezes in his miming gesture like a lamb suddenly facing a lion. "I'm living my dream," he replies with total panic and desperation again. "Stop it," the wife orders him.

The husband stops, scared stiff and mute. The commercial ends. The wife makes the ruling and that is the end of the story for the humiliated husband who likes to live his dream of becoming a mime.

Humour is supposedly the intention of these commercials, to sell their products. However, they are propagating women's assertiveness and men's passivity and subordination in relationships in the new era—which is largely true but not a proper viewpoint. They exploit the fact that men are put down by women and they cannot do a darn thing about it. They advocate women's power, all for the sake of flattering and encouraging them to buy their products.

742. These commercials reflect the reality of relationships, but also propagate arrogance. They find it funny that women's superiority is becoming a part of our emerging culture, including aggression toward men. How are we going to convince ourselves that these values are destructive for both

genders? How many years will we need to be convinced? Probably a century is a good guess!

743. If someone asks the author to identify the most destructive force damaging relationships, he would suggest 'Hollywood.' Those naïve love stories, senseless gender confrontations, and meaningless conclusions have been contaminating the brains of the public all over the world. Some ignorant writers are doing everybody a disservice by their unrealistic, simple-minded scripts. A scene in the movie *Two Weeks Notice* with Sandra Bullock and Hugh Grant is really confusing and interesting: Sometime in the middle of the night, Sandra is returning a pair of shoes that she had borrowed from her friend—a weird timing all by itself. After the friend goes down and opens the door, they sit down near the curb to talk. The friend's husband appears at the window of their apartment, looks down into the street with concern, and says, "Everything's okay?" The wife yells at him with unbelievable attitude, "Not now! Everything is not about you!" Her comment and tone of voice has no relevance and meaning in that scene or in the context of the whole movie. It only reflects the absurdity of relationships' atmosphere. "Okay," the husband mumbles with apprehension as he withdraws away from the window. Obviously, he would have been accused of apathy if he had not tried to find out if her wife were okay, because all he knew was that she had gone downstairs to answer the door that late at night.

744. Women's higher intuition leads to other obstacles too. First, it makes them hasty and adamant in their judgments. Second, it increases their tendency to see and feel things without too much communication. Often they believe they can somehow read their husbands' minds and detect the hidden

clues in their conversations. They also assume that their husbands have the same level of intuition to understand their wishes without communicating the ideas to them clearly. They say something and expect their husbands to read between the lines and grasp their intentions. Then they get surprised and frustrated when their husbands do not comprehend their messages. Often they actually believe that their husbands have gotten the message, but are refusing to accept it or do something about it. Women believe that men are (or should be) as careful and intuitive as they are. They do not recognize that men's lower intuitiveness cannot be helped. Besides, men's logic dictates their need for clear communication instead of guessing the meaning of a vague message.

745. Overall, women do not believe in, and actually resist, an open and detailed communication, maybe because they feel their husbands are not listening, anyway, or are not interested. However, women have also become oversensitive and react harshly when men cannot understand their vague messages. As noted above, women's intuition is filling the gap that hinders men's understanding of a message without full communication. Men require clarity and women resist it since they find it unnecessary and unromantic, or they stay vague merely out of spite occasionally too. They simply expect their husbands to understand their meanings and intentions. For example, a husband was complaining to the author that whenever his wife realized her mistake, she only tried to make up for it by preparing his favourite meal, buying him a pair of socks, or making some kind of an indirect gesture of these natures. However, she never apologized directly or admitted that she had made a mistake. She simply expected to get the matter resolved without acknowledging the problem or discussing it. He said that, without an open discussion about the problem and a sincere apology, the matter never got resolved in his mind and his wounds never

healed. Actually, he considered his wife's behaviour (i.e., the gesture of buying him a present or cooking a fine meal) another type of manipulation and rising arrogance.

746. Couples are unaware of the hurdles of finding a new companion after getting out of their existing relationships. They are naïvely too optimistic about their chances of finding a reasonable match, even in their older ages. This is in particular difficult for women who are seeking men of higher qualities after their past relationships fail. Accordingly, couples' problems and frustrations would keep increasing in their second and third relationships. The only exception is when one or both partners become somewhat passive in their new relationship.

747. Many smart couples learn to perceive and handle their relationships more practically despite all the forces in society to make them radical in their relationships. These couples prefer to deal with the imperfections of their existing relationships rather than a new one. This is because they get used to its flaws and their partners' shortfalls after many years of sharing both good memories and life's hardships together. They learn to bear their relationship flaws by always recalling its merits. They admit that both partners in almost all relationships are most likely annoyed by each other's quirks. They feel that bearing the imperfections of their existing relationship is easier than learning about, and accepting, the new imperfections of a stranger (a new companion) all of a sudden. Men are particularly lazy, too, to go through the hassle of finding a new companion if the existing relationship is not too bad.

748. People usually expect peace in a new relationship after tolerating their previous partners' imperfections. For men especially, staying lonely seems preferable to living with a person who brings different kinds of idiosyncrasies and childish demands. People hate learning new stuff and adjusting, especially at the later stages of their lives. With old

age, they need less sex and usually have less patience or incentives, anyway, while getting more grouchy and demanding too.

749. We seek relationships to relieve our loneliness, but soon find out the absurdity of our dreams and efforts, because relationships actually make us feel the ultimate depth of loneliness and helplessness.

750. Everybody is getting more defensive in their interactions with others due to their past relationships and the rising level of aggressiveness in society. This is, of course, an added psychological pressure in relationships. We speak with people and our partners with apprehension (superficially), in order to not trigger their defence mechanisms and start an argument. This situation keeps relationships too edgy and unnatural.

751. At the same time, while people try to appear calm and tactful, they are also becoming more aggressive and offensive in order to counterbalance other people's (or their partners') assertiveness; as the saying goes: the best defence is offence.

752. Often relationships get into trouble when partners are unhappy with themselves and the life they are leading. Therefore, they depress their partners with their attitude too. Often they blame their partners for their own career failures, unhappiness, boredom, or unfulfilled dreams. Sometimes, they nag at each other to conceal their own shortfalls, e.g., in socializing. Then they gradually hate each other because they believe that their partner is in fact responsible for their unhappiness.

753. Partners waste a lot of time and energy on faultfinding and blaming each other supposedly for the sake of improving their relationship. If only they realized that in the end, it does not matter whose fault the problems are as long as those problems remain irreconcilable!

754. The bottom line is that couples must either find mutually agreeable solutions (a suitable relationship model) to relate somehow or separate.
755. When relationship problems go beyond certain levels, the only solution is to find ways of relating (living together) passively at a lower level of the 'relationship needs tree' (model), and stop trying to solve the problems per se.
756. Relationship problems are often unsolvable, because they are caused by irreversible idiosyncrasies of partners. We humans have proven that not even our logic and common sense can help us solve our personal or social (including economic and political) problems.
757. The gender struggles to reach some illusory balance of power and equality is continuing at many levels, and the situation would most likely get out of hand in the future with global destructive outcomes.
758. We have difficulty learning from our mistakes and from the pains that our relationships are causing us. We prefer to suffer than change our perspective about the inherent limitations of relationships, especially within the context of the existing lifestyles.
759. Accordingly, it would be hard for the controversial messages of this book to find popularity amidst the mass of beautifully packaged messages (and social values) promising prosperity and happiness to everybody.
760. One of the main goals of a relationship framework is to bring *objectivity* back into relationships. However, a main hurdle is selling the idea of objectivity to women who are used to dealing with issues intuitively, and to men whose sense of logic has already made them dogmatic.
761. Nonetheless, society must gradually propagate the guidelines of a relationship framework. A more logical atmosphere must replace gender struggles for superiority. Reaching a balance of power and identity would require some

form of objectivity eventually. Otherwise, chaos would bring family relationships to a halt.

762. A puzzling point is, 'What kind of a partner are couples looking for when they insist on breaking each other's pride, mainly by competing with each other relentlessly?' In particular, a relevant question is, "Whether women can ever find submissive men attractive and trustworthy at all?" How could women enjoy or respect weak men?

763. Another major conflict is emerging: Couples are expecting their partners to be strong, competitive, and assertive outside the house to maximize families' welfare, but be submissive and passive at home to accommodate them.

764. The emerging trends in society, especially couples' needs for individuality and independence, are irreversible. People's psychological attributes and mentality due to gender differences cannot be changed either. Therefore, the only solution for our relationships is to find new mechanisms and relationship principles to match our new needs.

765. In addition, couples should get more serious about modifying their mindsets and viewing relationships in a more practical perspective. They should do so for increasing their chances of building a reliable relationship. We need a more productive relationship environment.

766. Partners' drive for independence leads to more distance between them. However, working within a relationship framework, while advocating partners' independence, rectifies this problem largely. Couples learn to respect and deal with their partners' need for independence and view 'independence' as a major requirement of teamwork. Meanwhile, more detailed mechanisms of teamwork must be developed too.

767. The irony is that hardly can anybody find his or her soul mate because of the way we behave nowadays. Even if we happen to find them by accident, we just keep losing them due to our phony personalities and ideologies, not to men-

tion our idiotic games and Egos. It is interesting that even couples with similar values, lifestyle, and priorities keep rejecting one another since they do not know how to relate effectively and naturally.

768. Some couples have indeed found their soul mates, but they lose them when their own oversensitivity gives them wrong impressions about the health of their relationship and the purpose of relationships in general. They lose their partners due to their fantasies, such as a better life with a different partner, love, money, etc. High expectations and misperceptions are making couples lose the soul mates they have already found.

769. Partners get too intimate too early as a sign of love, trust, and loyalty, instead of proving all of these high qualities gradually through real actions and right attitude. Often, partners actually try to manipulate each other by showing off a polished image of themselves. Nevertheless, statistics show that most couples end up losing their love, trust, and loyalty in their relationships.

770. Partners try to exploit each other (knowingly or inadvertently) by *activating their MLove to fake SLove to get ELove.*

771. People assume they are (or can be) loving, trustworthy, or loyal. However, all evidences indicate that humans are impure by nature, and then environment makes them even more cruel and aggressive.

772. Relationships suffer from humans' inherent defects more than anything else. Some artificial expressions of passion, as a result of attraction or other needs of partners, do not change their true nature as humans with all their inherent defects.

773. Our rampant relationship issues are causing more mistrust amongst youth. Thus, each generation is causing more damages for the relationships of the future generations. We are making our children more sceptical about marriage and

less prepared to deal with its requirements, especially its most likely consequence, i.e., separation.

774. Driven by the recent popular ideologies, including positive thinking slogans, people like to believe that life is beautiful and that happiness is within reach. Yet, most prominent philosophies and our personal experiences indicate the opposite: That life is nothing but a place for suffering and paying for our past or present sins. The point is that our idealism and search for this phantom happiness are misleading many couples; they just put too much demand on each other recklessly and then finally separate.

775. It is a pity that our misguided perceptions stop us from taking advantage of our only opportunity to suffer less in this world: That is, by bringing more objectivity into our relationships and enjoying one another, instead of arguing about our inconsequential needs and obsessions, especially this illusive 'happiness.' We are actually proving the philosophers right about life being only a place for suffering. For one thing, we suffer from our relationships (or lack of them) due to our own naïve expectations and games.

776. Being optimistic and positive about life are useful tools. However, when they cause gross misperceptions and raise our naïve expectations, e.g., for more love or a better partner, they must be construed as another cause of partners' confusion and relationship failures.

777. The bottom line is that if positive thinking and 'living in the now' schemes worked, by now everybody would have joined in to reap their rewards. Everybody would have benefited from these magical cures by now and we could see all those happy faces around us.

778. However, all we see nowadays is more depression and desperation. We need the highest level of antidepressants to help us continue living and suffering. If positive thinking and 'living in the now' schemes worked, relationship problems had disappeared and everybody was living happily

with their soul mates. Instead, we see more unrealizable expectations and self-pity.

779. Many people are edgy these days because their positive thinking alone, even when they combine it with a great deal of personal efforts, does not seem to help them. They still lose their companions to the phony life philosophies that are misleading people, and they still lose their life savings in financial markets because of other people's greed or incompetence.

780. Many philosophers suggest that life cannot be a happy affair, because the minute we have nothing to do, and can supposedly enjoy life, we get bored. Therefore, we look for adventure, work, or a new companion to rejuvenate our lives. However, they all make us suffer, too, especially our relationships.

781. In all, we struggle all our lives to find something creative to do or a worthy companion to give us some moments of happiness. Some spiritualists, of course, believe that we could help ourselves a little if we learned to be a better human being and stayed content, which is a tough mission for most of us.

782. Nowadays, being a good human does not always pay off anyway. He/she is often perceived as a weak and passive individual and not taken seriously. It might not help (actually damage) his/her relationship, anyway, if his/her partner is not an equally good human being. Therefore, being a good person may not be necessarily useful for drawing other people's compassion or achieving tangible benefits.

783. The only benefit of being good is to mitigate one's suffering and possibly get a better chance to relate to one's partner unselfishly.

PART III

Our Choices

Chapter Twelve
Relationship Solutions

Relationship problems are too complex and widespread to overcome quickly. However, what makes the situation obscure and most frustrating is our unwillingness to even acknowledge that this pandemic has deep-seated roots, which can be remedied only by radical changes. With this kind of passive mindset, we are not making systematic efforts to explore the underlying hurdles of relationships. Our passivity about the existing chaos and the complexity of the relationship environment are the main reasons why it will take at least a century to find real solutions for relationships. On the other hand, we have some viable options to improve our relationships immediately by making some minor changes in our mentalities.

Knowing the basic nature of relationships from the discussions in the previous chapters, we have three choices:

A. **Continue with the status quo**, hoping that Nature will take its course and eventually a format will emerge for relationships. Meanwhile, there will be more separations, conflicts, and paranoia about relationships. And there is no way to predict the outcome. The chance that a logical and

efficient framework evolves out of this chaos is terribly slim.
B. **Hope that one gender will eventually dominate the other** so that order may return to relationships. It is a fact that humans have difficulty relating to one another, and to work as a team in the long run, especially the opposite sexes. This is truer nowadays with individualism, arrogance, and greed satiating our mentality and social values. However, the option of one gender taking the superior role in relationships would not work in the long run either. Chaos and equality struggles would continue to overwhelm relationships.
C. **Create and propagate a relationship framework** to guide couples run their relationships smoothly and relate efficiently. With the increasing complexity of society, the longevity of relationships might be doomed anyway. However, a flexible and modern relationship framework could at least anticipate, and prepare couples for, the high likelihood that relationships in the new era would fail.

Hopefully, the third option would appeal to most of us. It would minimize the amount of frictions between partners and improve social atmosphere drastically too. In addition, couples would be better prepared to deal with the reality of separation and living independently. Anyway, this book advocates the third option, as the author believes it would provide the only solution for relationships.

As the first step for finding 'Relationship Solutions', we must return to the dozen **facts** emphasized at the end of Chapter One (and listed on the opposite page as bottom line too) and deal with them proactively. We have a choice to do something about these facts now or just wait until the relationship environment faces a total chaos. The bottom line is that we have only limited choices to make our relationships work. On the other hand, we have a great opportunity to really study and consider our choices wisely. The bottom line is that we must:

A: Upgrade our mindset and acknowledge that:
- Both our initial optimism about relationships (when we start one) and subsequent retaliations (when it fails) are destructive.
- Our perspective of relationships is too naïve, unrealistic, and incompatible with the format of modern society. We must learn to lower our expectations from relationships in order to attend to our increasing personal needs independently.
- We must prepare ourselves, both emotionally and financially, to deal with the high possibility of failure in our marriages and relationships.
- Only by conscious efforts and major personal sacrifices, a relationship can be sustained on a long-term basis. Our present mindset (personal priorities) and social values make the job of prolonging our relationships extremely difficult, if not impossible altogether.

B. Understand human limitations and respect the fact that:
- The complexity of human cognition and behaviour, driven by a variety of personal needs, traits, and perceptions, causes all kinds of relationship problems.
- The underlying causes of relationship failures remain beyond partners' control. In other words, partners cannot help the situation. They are helpless due to human's psychological defects and genetic built.
- Our faultfinding attitude toward our partners is a futile exercise. Furthermore, our efforts to change others (our partners) are absurd, especially when the matter is pursued through retaliation and intimidation.

C. Develop new relationship mechanisms and guidelines
mainly by admitting that:
- Dynamic relationship principles are needed to reflect the realities of the modern world.
- New guidelines are needed to facilitate individuals' drive to be independent, assertive, proactive, and make the best use of their lives.
- Revolutionary social mechanisms and norms are needed to help us manage our relationships and possibly reduce the chances of failure.
- Revolutionary laws must be devised to make separations easy.
- Revolutionary social mechanisms and education (especially at high school) are needed to prepare couples for the psychological effects of relationships, especially separation.

Making tough choices outside the box, usually against the social norms would not be easy, but we have no other option. Thus, the first thing we must do is to change our mindset about relationships.

784. The main mental adjustments required for couples are:

a) Partners must reduce their expectations from relationships drastically.
b) Partners must know the specific relationship needs* before entering relationships. They must also be mentally equipped and willing to observe these relationship needs and guidelines.
c) Partners must learn, and be willing, to relate to each other within the boundaries of the relationship framework*. They must identify the relationship model that best fits their personal needs and personalities*.

d) Partners should view relationships a temporary arrangement, unless they do all the right things (which would be somewhat unlikely for most people).
e) Partners should be prepared to leave their relationships with open mind, without fuss or retaliation and before they start to hate each other.
f) Partners should view their relationship as an independent entity like a business enterprise. The concept of R-entity.
g) Couples should not look up to the government to resolve their relationship squabbles. Rather, they should depend on their initial contracts that outline their commitments to one another at the outset.
h) Couples should remember that love, ethics, and religion are not reliable mechanisms for authenticating or protecting their relationships. The vows exchanged in those settings are good only for glamorizing our feelings and ceremonies.

* Discussing the details of the following important topics is beyond the scope of this book:
  - Relationship Needs
  - Relationship Expectations
  - Relationship Framework
  - Relationship Guidelines
  - Relationship Models
  - Relationship Success Factors

Interested readers are encouraged to read about them in *The Nature of Love and Relationships* or in *Relationship Needs, Framework, and Models*.

In line with the above mental adjustments, we have the following choices to see relationships in a more progressive and realistic light.

785. Traditionally, we have viewed relationships as a reliable, manageable, sweet arrangement that can satisfy many of our personal needs in addition to companionship. However, nowadays, the likelihood of any relationship failing is much higher than succeeding. This is an obvious observation judging by the percentage of divorces and the turmoil of dragging relationships.
786. This means that, as logical people, we should make major adjustments in our mentality to suddenly view relationships as a temporary arrangement, unless we are smart and lucky enough to make it work on a long-term basis.
787. Now couples must be able to prove that they deserve to stay in their relationships. They carry a high burden of proof (by demonstrating their aptitude) for prolonging their relationships beyond the initial romance and as partners' patience begins to falter.
788. One major misperception in society and people's minds is that relationships should last forever. This naïve expectation comes from our traditional mentality. Nowadays, however, this is the least likely scenario considering the statistics on divorce, family problems, strive for individualism, sexuality, and the increasing level of stress in society. So now, we must perceive relationships more in terms of an open-ended arrangement rather than a long-term commitment.
789. Naturally, this condition (to view relationships as a temporary arrangement) appears like a major setback in terms of relationships' success and value. The readers might ask, "How could this seemingly negative mindset lead to the success of relationships?" The answer is that for solving the hectic situation of relationships, we must face reality somehow. This awakening would actually help the state of relationships enormously as explained in the next point.
790. In the author's opinion, we should indeed look forward with great excitement to implement this new mentality and approach about the high vulnerability of our relationships. The

reason is that the advantages of such a mentality might amaze us in the end. This would prove to be one of those unique instances where reverse psychology would prove to work extremely well. The couples' knowledge that their relationship would terminate *automatically*, at a certain point, would make them stay together much longer than would be under the present circumstance. They simply stay vigilant and protect their relationship in a constructive, teamwork environment. They realize that they must work on their relationship regularly to maintain it instead of taking it for granted and letting it expire at a preset date. This reverse psychology would definitely help our societies in at least four ways:

- Couples get into their relationships more carefully based on intelligent analyses of their needs, their compatibility, and the suitability of a particular relationship model for them.
- Couples work harder and more consciously to prolong their relationships instead of allowing it to expire. This would most likely increase the longevity of most relationships that are worth saving.
- Couples are mentally prepared to leave their relationships with the least amount of shock and hassle when a relationship is not working. They know from the beginning that, if necessary, separation is a good and acceptable possibility.
- Ending relationships is automatic and hassle free.

791. Nevertheless, making such a harsh mental adjustment—to view relationships as a temporary arrangement—would be difficult for people. Therefore, it will take time to get there.

792. At the same time, people's present attitude indicates that they somehow handle their marriages as a temporary arrangement, anyway. They are too eager to abandon their relationships, unless partners' dire expectations are met and

they feel happy according to their demanding and calculating minds.
793. Although the longevity of relationships has many advantages if it can be properly mastered, three main questions can be asked:
- Are humans instinctually equipped to live together for the length of their long lives (especially now that life expectancy is increasing so drastically)?
- Do partners' personalities and needs support the possibility of living together forever?
- Do our new social values and settings encourage the possibility of relationship longevity?

794. The author explains and argues in his book, *The Nature of Love and Relationships* that the answer to all the three above questions is no.
795. One clue that humans are not instinctually programmed to live together permanently is their amazing craving for sexual freedom. The urge to experience sex with many partners is in almost all human beings. As a means of happiness or psychological remedy, sex has also become too important for us to remain content with only one partner. Sex is also the first refuge we seek when our relationships face a calamity.
796. Another major hurdle for relationship longevity is that humans have to struggle hard to get along, especially the opposite sexes.
797. In all, it seems that humans are inherently not made to be in lasting relationships.
798. A good portion of people has even less capacity (including patience) to be in relationships due to their intense self-centredness and deep idiosyncrasies. Yet, we all try to force the idea of longevity out of habit, loneliness, urge for procreation, etc.

799. Nevertheless, couples' mental adjustment is necessary for all the reasons discussed in this book. One main objective is to make people more conscious and careful about the true nature of relationships in the new era. They must get more realistic and view relationships with open eyes and minds—not by the way they feel and hope for. Most people are actually doing this already, though in an incomplete way. They assess the financial prospects of their relationships furtively, but do not wish to admit its importance or express it openly. They do not want to be accused of being calculating and unromantic when they are starting a relationship. Nonetheless, we must act according to the statistics and vivid experiences around us.
800. We must now admit this fact openly and prepare ourselves (both financially and emotionally) for viewing relationships as a temporary arrangement. In all, the concept might appear too radical, if not vulgar, and it may turn off many readers already. However, considering all the facts, trends, and choices discussed in this book, the readers may feel more supportive of the need for a progressive mentality and other radical points offered in Chapter Fourteen.
801. Obviously, it is unromantic and depressing to start our relationships on a seemingly wrong foot, with a seemingly negative attitude. However, being realistic at the outset may save us nervous breakdowns and separation hassles.
802. The challenges of separation seem inevitable for a majority of relationships and it pays off to be prepared for them.
803. Learning about the deep roots of relationship failures would also help us realize that they are the symptoms of social changes that we have not adapted ourselves to. Therefore, partners' retaliation out of spite cannot correct anything. Retaliating to make our partners change is not going to work either. It merely reflects our own utmost immaturity and wishful thinking.

804. As noted before, one objective of this book is to pinpoint the high vulnerability of relationships in modern societies. Low longevity is one of its obvious vulnerabilities. Yet, with a more realistic perception about this most likely outcome of relationships, we would have a more rational state of mind when things start going wrong and react more constructively. On the other hand, this heightened awareness might actually induce enough incentives and sincere efforts by us to save our relationships.

805. Learning about the inherent causes of relationship problems might help those who are smart and humble to adopt a constructive role for managing their relationships. Adopting some relationship principles, as suggested in this book, is also for the same purpose, i.e., to make couples relate more effectively.

806. Knowing about the complexity of human behaviour and its adverse effects on their relationships is the only remedy left to save couples. We should reconsider our view of relationships, redefine our expectations realistically, and be prepared for the worst scenario, i.e., separation.

Appendix 12-A
Personality Aspects' Properties

As a main step for revamping our mentality about relationships, we must grasp our personality flaws and make proper adjustments. We have many choices in terms of understanding and making better use of our personality aspects as explained in this appendix.

807. As a potent solution for our ailing relationships, we can learn about, and apply, our personality aspects more actively and effectively. We can make a habit of monitoring and distinguishing the personality aspects in our encounters. We can be the best judge as to which one of our personality aspects is in control during an event or communication. We sometimes do this assessment after the communication is completed. Sometimes we feel sorry for what we said. We might go back and at least try to correct our past mistakes. Often, however, Ego stops us even from correcting our mistakes, i.e., by apologizing at least. Nonetheless, the most effective method would be to assess the tone and content of our messages in advance.

808. Especially, we can make an effort to use Self more often to soothe someone's hurt feelings. We know how to do this and probably do it occasionally. Therefore, it is possible to use Self more often if we just push ourselves to be a little more conscious of the personality aspect that is trying to dominate a message.

809. After we do this simple exercise for a while, we begin to notice our awareness level enhancing gradually. This awareness helps us notice and improve our habits, and attain the tranquility we crave all our lives. Of course, changing our habits and personality is not a straightforward matter. It does not occur easily and quickly. Still, the mere

sense of committing to a self-awareness regimen is crucial for overcoming the difficulties of changing ourselves and perhaps the people around us. Keeping track of the interworking and manifestation of our personality aspects is the most important step toward self-awareness.

810. Committing oneself to such a noble regimen is difficult because we must keep fighting our Ego without any tangible incentive. Attaining tranquility is the only incentive for self-awareness and personality change. This is a major incentive, though, if we really wish to find peace and happiness. This is the best way to enjoy a sense of relative freedom from social burdens and we might even start to enjoy our relationships.

811. Obviously, breaking the rules of social belonging to build Self appears too naïve and ridiculous. How can we ignore the tangible rewards of social compliance like wealth, sex, and power, all in pursuit of tranquility and freedom? These states appear to be abstract concepts and wishful thinking after all. For all these reasons, a person must truly feel the need to change the direction of his/her life, and then gain the needed courage and commitment for pursuing the path of self-awareness. Some people come to this realization when they face life hurdles and hit the tall wall of disappointments, especially in their relationships. Even then, they require special wisdom to realize the need for an alternative lifestyle. Only this wisdom and their devotion might help them learn about Self and move on the path to self-awareness.

812. As noted before, all the three personality aspects have both good and bad qualities. It is true that Ego causes more trouble and leads to badness more often than the other personality aspects. However, Ego contributes highly to our welfare in so many ways, too, especially for boosting our confidence and managing our defence mechanisms.

813. On the other hand, Self could cause trouble and badness too. For example, instincts make us believe in certain ways or beliefs that are no longer applicable in our complex society. For example, imagine making investments based on trust or intuition rather than doing due diligence and studying all the risks and alternatives before committing ourselves. Marriages in the past worked nicely simply based on couples' trust and traditional habits. However, society is now too complex to choose a spouse and live with him/her before years of searching and contemplating.

814. It is not necessarily a good thing that we have been forced to be analytical and indecisive, but we have reached this point by the force of history. Our sense of spirituality, which is a pure symbol of Self, is nowadays tainted, too, by all kinds of religious fanaticism and major corruption of clergies. Therefore, Self has its weaknesses for adapting to the newer social needs and survival.

815. The problems with Model are numerous, too, and beyond the scope of our discussions in this book. For one thing, Model has made people phony and calculating and we have a hard job separating true compassion from fake ones. The manipulating power of Model is infecting our lives and minds. We do not even believe the words of our leaders in politics, economics, or religion. They keep disappointing us out of stupidity, sheer arrogance, and hypocrisy.

816. Even in smaller scales, the problem with Model is that people can read our fake pretences if we are not good at playing the role. This causes more mistrust, frictions, and resistance because people want to challenge our phony personality. Although many gullible people buy phony pretences, the task of making Model look convincing is tough nowadays. Everybody is becoming more sceptical about other people's attitudes and words. Instead of trust, we now mistrust one another unless proven otherwise.

817. Model is too prevalent in modern societies, which means people are manipulating or cheating one another more than ever. Everybody is trying to show-off and portray an image of themselves that is quite unauthentic. At the same time, they must try hard to be convincing too. Their lies and deceits must remain hidden. This is hard, though, since everybody is learning to discount people's pretences, and because the trust level is declining fast in society.

818. Relationship problems are particularly attributed to personality clashes between partners. However, most people are unaware of the roots of personality clashes. They are insensitive about the interworking of their personality aspects. And of course they ignore the fact that they and their partners cannot change their personalities at will. People's unique personalities cannot be changed easily. Only awareness, partners' goodwill, and gradual modifications through Self and Model may help them save their relationships.

819. Using Model might resemble the role-playing methods prescribed by marriage counsellors. However, there is a fundamental difference between these two approaches. Using Model, for improving ourselves, would be based on partners' true conviction to learn about, and manage, their personality aspects. The idea is not to express love or behave in certain ways artificially just to satisfy one's partner. Rather, the idea is to learn about (and manage) one's personality flaws. Model is used to play artificial roles or authentic ones, of course. Model may cause damage if it plays artificial roles, but it becomes useful when it is used to reinforce our authentic needs.

Self-awareness for Boosting Our Relationships

A useful process of self-awareness and also minimizing relationship clashes is to pursue the following steps:

A. Monitor your behaviour in terms of personality aspects regularly. Learn how each aspect of your personality is driven by some motives or impulses and then find out what they are. You may use the list of the motives in Appendix 4-A as a general guide.
B. Assess the integrity of your motives and decide if they are suitable for an enlightened person who does not need to play games or retaliate. Apply Self and Model to curb your selfish motives and improve your tactics for managing your daily routines.
C. After gaining enough self-awareness, monitor your partner's behaviour in terms of his/her personality aspects. The objective is to see how your partner is helpless in the face of his/her forceful personality aspects. Note his/her helplessness to change his/her behaviour. Remember that personality aspects, e.g., Ego, are triggered by inner forces (instincts, genetic, habits, impulses) and external forces. Instead of criticizing him/her for his/her flaws, see if you can help him/her follow a self-awareness routine too (mainly by observing his/her own personality aspects).
D. If impossible to tolerate your partner, or if you are unable to convince him/her to pursue a self-awareness approach, stop your useless struggles to save an irreconcilable relationship. Either learn to live with his/her imperfections or get out of the relationship in a most civilized and hassle-free manner. Stop retaliating and arguing.
E. Even when both partners have some level of self-awareness and knowledge of the personality aspects, building relationships requires a continuous monitoring of the 'personality aspect clashes' during partners' encounters, and then making proper modifications along the way. Furthermore, couples must satisfy all the other needs of relationships, too, mainly the matter of choosing the right relationship model for them. An important role of a proper re-

lationship model is to minimize the frequency of clashes between partners' two sets of personality aspects.

Chapter Thirteen
Relationship Guidelines

Some implied *principles* used to help humans manage their relationships, until recently. Whether it was tribal, religious, or cultural norms, some form of ethics and etiquettes prevailed. Those values, ordinarily informal but clear, guided couples to live in some form of harmony. Obviously, those outmoded types of family structures are no longer applicable or useful in new societies. However, the question is whether people can live without some form of norms or principles to keep the families in a relatively coherent and manageable harmony in the new world. The answer in the author's opinion is a resounding NO. Thus, the objective in this book has been to develop a means of returning order and harmony to relationships, despite the gloomy prospect nowadays to succeed in this endeavour.

Starting perhaps only half a century ago, suddenly all the old relationship principles have gradually eroded along with the advent of so-called progressive societies and mentalities. Those old principles have become obsolete considering the emergence of new lifestyles, women's new role in organizations and society, and other symptoms of human struggle to prove his independence and spirit. Personalities have changed and people have become more complex without any expertise about dealing with one another effectively. Individuals' needs have skyrocketed and their expectations from life and relationships have increased, yet their patience and morality have declined drastically. We have propagated arrogance, extravagance, sexuality, weird life philosophies, and unlimited artificial needs.

Now we stand at the junction of history. We do not know how to relate to one another emotionally, effectively, and efficiently. Thus, we suffer from our substandard relationships. Our agony heightens daily because we ignore the current cultural deficiencies. We are unaware of the hazards that the lack of relationship principles has caused. The aggravating hurdles of relationships, mainly due to mounting personal idiosyncrasies, are affecting all of us directly and fiercely while social complexities increase too. Our interactions, at work, at home, or with friends, have become less sincere and manageable in all respects. Family relationships, in particular, have suffered both in terms of child rearing and couples' ability to relate in their relationships. The absence of some kind of principles to guide partners is hindering the job of relating in relationships. Partners' oversensitivity and subjectivity are shortening the longevity of relationships nowadays. In all, there are no Generally Acceptable Relationship Principles (GARP) to guide couples.

We have a choice and obligation as individuals and society as a whole to introduce GARP and emphasize on its main principles as briefly noted below:

820. Viewing 'relationships' as an independent entity (R-entity), like a business enterprise, does not undermine its emotional importance.
821. R-entity is only a concept with the important task of reminding couples that relationship needs are unique and not an extension of their personal needs.

822. R-entity can be viewed as an important third party (the third leg of a tripod) in relationships to keep partners stable and objective.
823. A marital partnership is many folds more complex and demanding than any business partnership, because the cost of failure is much higher.
824. R-entity simply provides the opportunity of bringing a similar level of discipline that exists in business to the concept we call *relationships*.
825. We are all facing major dilemmas in life because: 1) Relationships are now too complex, 2) we need companions more urgently than ever, 3) we have become less patient, and 4) we are too obsessed with love and an idealistic perception of relationships in the new era.
826. Suddenly, our level of patience has become too low, especially in relationships, because we have not still determined the acceptable level of tolerance, and because we have kept rising our expectations from relationships.
827. We do not realize that, in fact, we have created more limitations for our relationships by our exaggerated perception of its high potential, especially in terms of bringing us happiness.
828. Our options about relationships seem to be clear. They are:
    - Keep fighting and struggling in relationships, or live in solitude, while sticking to some rigid perceptions of an ideal relationship.
    - Learn to accept the new reality about relationships, reduce expectations from them, fulfil as much of personal needs outside the relationship, tolerate some level of relationship imperfections, and separate peacefully when the relationship proves unmanageable.
829. The ultimate objective of a relationship framework and a set of principles is to *enable partners relate to each other emotionally, effectively, and efficiently (the three Es)* even when

a variety of their personal expectations cannot be fulfilled in their relationship.
830. Relating emotionally does not mean love. Rather, it means understanding other people's limitations, inherent hurts, and inability to change, and our capacity to still show sympathy toward them.
831. People are oversensitive but lack compassion. Often they are careless and heartless themselves, but are hurt by the simplest comments or imagining inadequate attention. This is of course a symptom of their high Ego too.
832. The complexity of relationships is easy to grasp when we appreciate the complexity of human nature. We must realize how hopelessly helpless we are due to our psychological defects and idiosyncrasies.
833. Relationships would always remain a demanding and confusing aspect of our lives. Accordingly, we must begin to see and accept relationships in a different light, as a temporary union. And we should also learn to become humbler humans and modify our life values.
834. Not having a relationship sounds ridiculous to a large majority of the population who seeks a companion as a basic need. Both our instincts and culture constantly force us to attend to this need actively.
835. In all, we must modify our mindset to deal with the relationships' specific demands. The particular relationship model that couples choose should keep their affairs and communications manageable, while allowing them to deal with their personal needs individually.
836. A couple relates actively when they can maintain positive emotions, effectiveness, and efficiency in their relationship—the three Es.
837. Couples relate passively when they learn to live with minimum expectations from their relationship while it still remains manageable and functional. The three Es are somewhat necessary in 'passive relating' too.

838. It is important for partners to know about the way they are 'relating,' if at all, and acknowledge it too.
839. The absence of some kind of relationship principles (GARP) is preventing partners to relate. This is a frustrating shortfall of relationships nowadays.
840. GARP will be an easy-to-read document for the public. It will list all the facts and guidelines about relationships according to the social setting of the time.
841. A replica of GARP is available in the books, *the Nature of Love and Relationships* and *Relationship Needs, Framework, and Models* by this author.
842. GARP's objectives are explained in Appendix 13-A at the end of this chapter.
843. GARP can help partners understand and respect each other's boundaries. In addition, couples need GARP to recognize how humans' inherent shortfalls are affecting their behaviour. Unfortunately, the present state of relationships is mostly dominated by partners' phony roles, games, and retaliations—instead of being managed by GARP.
844. The bottom line is that we must be willing to sacrifice in some respects to gain the tranquility of manageable relationships, and we must learn how to tame our Egos to accept and honour GARP.
845. GARP is urgently needed because couples are unaware of the scope of conflicts that their demand for large levels of both dependence and independence has created in their relationships.
846. The process of implementing GARP would require a lot of learning and adjusting. This would take time and patience.
847. Logically, a fair and sensible GARP should be adopted quickly by everybody for their own benefit. However, overcoming old habits and urges to entertain GARP or other relationship mechanisms would be difficult.
848. Convincing people to replace their emotional decision processes with GARP would be difficult.

849. GARP might appear doomed at the outset by its attempt to introduce reasoning and formulate some principles about relationships. Reasoning in the emotional environment of relationships sounds too absurd.
850. GARP appears like a bizarre approach in a society where objectivity and logic seem to have lost their meanings a long time ago.
851. Nonetheless, the idea of introducing GARP appears to be the only option left for society to reverse the deteriorating state of relationships.
852. Most of us, with a manageable amount of psychological defects and destructive urges, eventually appreciate the potential of GARP. We must become more open-minded and realistic about our expectations from relationships by adopting GARP.
853. We must identify a practical balance between couples' personal needs and the relationship needs in the new era and define those boundaries in GARP.
854. Once a platform is defined and accepted by prominent sociologists, psychologists, and the public, modifying and expanding GARP would be an automatic process like all other social processes in progressive societies of the future.
855. Scholars and experts must find creative ways to inform the public of the flaws of our existing ways. They must do more research and be more proactive in terms of changing couples' mindsets about relationships.
856. As human beings, with the objective of reaching our deep potentials and tranquility, we are wasting too much time and energy on the petty problems of relationships. This is absurd and a sin.
857. Partners usually question each other's logic regarding their relationship approaches and needs and ask each other "Who said that?" GARP can provide a point of reference (an authority) for many of those questionable personal preferences that partners find arbitrary at the present time.

858. Obviously, the suggestions in this book have no value for those readers who believe the situation with relationships is fine as it is. However, for those of us who are tired of the existing atmosphere, we must prepare ourselves for drastic changes if we are really looking for tangible results.

859. The bottom line is that we need a framework to redefine relationships and reassess socioeconomic conditions in our modern society.

860. Unfortunately, it appears that only radical solutions might reverse the fast-deteriorating state of relationships.

861. In the present atmosphere, the main thoughts for any person looking for a companion should be: 1) Do both partners grasp the intricacies and risks of relationships, 2) have they developed the right mindset for facing the inevitable setbacks, and 3) are they enough mature, independent, and strong to deal with both the inevitable headaches of being in a relationship and when it falls apart.

Appendix 13-A
GARP's Objectives

The dozen main objectives of GARP are listed below:

1. *GARP can help us* **capture and propagate the main features of a successful relationship.** It can show how a relationship may thrive, what it is supposed to achieve, and what we can expect from it. GARP will provide the list of success factors in relationships too. Accordingly, GARP replaces the arbitrary (subjective) criteria that couples use nowadays for running their relationships or assessing its viability. This will bring objectivity back into relationships.
2. *GARP can help us* **realize our psychological limitations as human beings.** It can show how our personal limitations cause relationship problems. GARP can enhance our sensitivity toward our partners, reduce our expectations from them, and mitigate our resentment about the substandard environment of relationships.
3. *GARP can help us* **realize why individuals' psychological defects are not easily repairable.** It will emphasize that we must find the means of circumventing those defects as much as possible instead of criticizing them. Some of the ideas discussed in this book regarding human psychology can be adopted as *principles* and included in GARP. For example, we can agree that, as a plausible principle, 'People can hardly change themselves.' One reason is that for a person to change, he/she must change his/her cognition, which in return requires accessing the depth of his/her unconscious. He/she must draw upon some extraordinary energy and spirituality to become a better human. A principle in GARP may reflect that 'The positive thinking methods, which attempt to give people a power to change themselves and improve their lives, would hardly provide the deep conviction and gradual enlightenment required for

change.' Only ongoing meditation and realization, to grasp our Self more tangibly, might help.
4. *GARP can help us* **realize that couple's need for independence cannot and should not be restricted in relationships.** The new models and principles of relationships should be built around one fundamental fact: That majority of people nowadays find the highest social value in personal independence. This is a prevalent perspective after the advent of the women's lib movement and race equality struggles. Despite the inherent perception of dependence in relationships, as well as humans' instinctual need for dependence, our desire for independence is overwhelming every thought and action we engage in nowadays. Therefore, GARP should advocate this general trend that is preoccupying people. But then, for pursuing this basic principle consistently, there is a high demand on people to plan their personal lives as independently as possible, especially in their relationships. This includes maintaining financial independence, while respecting the spirit of cooperation and teamwork in their relationships more than ever.
5. *GARP can help us* **realize that a dysfunctional relationship must be terminated civilly and easily.** To insist on correcting the inherent personality flaws of our partners, or retaliating relentlessly to make them suffer, is futile and childish. Once we believe in GARP's objectives and the other facts discussed throughout this book, we appreciate our partners' helplessness in terms of their personality flaws and perceptions. With this mindset, we might at last realize the futility of our lifelong struggle to either change our partners to suit our needs, or retaliate in order to make them suffer the way they make us suffer. Partners may realize that adhering to GARP and treating relationships objectively are beyond their patience or capacity. In that case, they must courageously submit to a friendly separation.

Ending unmanageable relationships should be a natural and automatic process.
6. *GARP can help us* **realize that the focus for correcting relationship conflicts is not our partner but ourselves.** As stated repeatedly in this book, the only way to make relationships work is by having each partner work on his/her own flaws individually and honestly. They must commit themselves to become a better person regardless of its benefits for the relationship. A partner's decision to be a better person and how to pursue this impossible mission is a personal matter and challenge. Partners should not pressure each other to become a better person to save their relationship. It would not work this way. It requires personal conviction, which cannot be forced upon someone. A decision to change lies only in the hands of each partner.

The goal of self-awareness is to prepare a partner to curb his/her Ego, tolerate relationship flaws better, and accept his/her partner's shortfalls easier, unless the situation deteriorates beyond tolerance.

7. *GARP can help us* **create a means of dealing with our relationships without the need to depend on government or religious rules.** The more comprehensive GARP becomes, and the more it is universally accepted by couples, the less people need the government or religious rules to interfere with their relationships. The clarity of GARP should help couples discuss their relationship bottlenecks objectively and judge the possibility of saving it or terminating it. Relationships start based on goodwill and optimism, yet we may get tired of our partner and wish to leave him or her, which is a natural reaction and must be honoured by everybody. However, the main cause of separations nowadays is the lack of principles to guide relationships and to measure their health regularly. If GARP can fill this gap, there would be no need to depend on bureaucratic, expensive, and time-consuming processes of gov-

ernments to resolve our differences and facilitate separation.
8. *GARP can help us* **establish relationship norms that fit the socioeconomic profile of the new era.** It must also remain dynamic and be modified as humanity progresses into more complex environments. All the evidences indicate that life and lifestyles will get horrifically complex for so many reasons. This is true even if we adopt an optimistic viewpoint and imagine that we would not destroy humanity and the Earth altogether within a few centuries. Nonetheless, GARP should fit the requirements of the time. And it must be dynamic and progressive in order to be effective. For example, partners' need for independence is a main theme of the present era. It has been only a few decades since we, especially women, have become adamant about independence. It has now been integrated within all facets of social life, including relationships. Many other psychological developments and structural changes have occurred in society, including our expanding appetite for compassion and consumption, and children's prominent role and demands in family life. They all affect the format of GARP, but nothing overwhelms GARP's theme in the 21st century as much as partners' unrelenting demands for identity and independence do. Nobody can say with certainty that in a century or so we will not feel exactly the opposite, i.e., demand dependence more heroically. People may finally realize that for real compassion they need to establish some rules of dependence. Suddenly dependence might become the new reality as much as independence is nowadays. This would actually be a rational progression that the author believes will happen. It would reflect a higher level of human maturity, which is a possibility, although so remote.

As discussed in Chapter Two, couples are still not quite aware of the conflict that their prominent demand for individualism has brought about. They are unaware of the scope of conflict that their demand for large levels of both dependence and independence has created in their relationships. They subtly expect relationships to satisfy their need for dependency while they pretend and shout independence publicly. The implicit urge for dependence, while insisting on independence explicitly and noisily, is one of the major hurdles in relationships in the new era. The sad realization we all must face is that we cannot have it both ways; to eat our cake and have it too.

9. *GARP can help us* **provide the guidelines for couple's teamwork.** GARP must be somewhat proactive in terms of suggesting the basic models and principles of teamwork and negotiating. In fact, GARP must be developed with the intention of enforcing teamwork. Couples need tools to help them deal with a large variety of conflicts in relationships. Instead of suggesting all kinds of untested models or ideas, however, GARP's initial guidelines must remain general and flexible while more precise ones are developed and tested gradually. It would take a few decades before a well-crafted set of guidelines, especially for teamwork, is developed by experts and made available to couples.

10. *GARP can help us* **choose the right relationship model and pinpoint the factors of compatibility between couples in order to minimize mismatches.** Based on their personality and needs, partners can choose the right model of relationship for them by using GARP's guidelines. These guidelines might also pinpoint the areas of potential conflicts between partners according to the relationship model chosen. Instead of looking for compatibility factors, as is the trend presently, GARP may suggest only those principles that can help couples *relate* effectively within the context of their relationship. Preventing mismatches in relationships and pinpointing the areas that conflicts could arise is another objective of GARP. This is different from

the task of finding compatible partners. The existing compatibility tests have so far proven inadequate for developing effective relationships.

11. *GARP can help us* **work within a uniform framework to assess our relationships and communicate objectively.** Psychologists and marriage counsellors can communicate amongst themselves according to these guidelines instead of offering a variety of personal or unproven methods. The existing techniques are not focused enough in terms of tackling the roots of relationship problems. Therefore, another objective of GARP is to create a uniform framework and language for psychologists and counsellors. Uniformity would not only make the diagnosis and treatment of relationship conflicts easier and transferable amongst experts, but also reduce the level of confusion and frustration for couples when each expert suggests something different and none of them works anyway. Couples are already suffering from their relationship conflicts and they do not need to be confused even more. They need a universally tested system to help them one way or another.

12. *GARP can help us* **view *relationships* as an independent, unique entity larger than the sum of the two individuals in it.** R-entity, as a fundamental principle by itself, has to be included in GARP. The idea is to bring objectivity into relationships instead of depending on subjective and unrealistic impressions of couples to define their relationships. Various characteristics of R-entity are listed in GARP for clarity and application. However, other principles listed in GARP would support R-entity as well. R-entity is the nucleus for developing the relationship framework and related concepts. It is the conceptual platform for us to make our relationships thrive.

Chapter Fourteen
Government Role and Legal System

In recent decades, laws and social mechanisms have been modified to deal only with the *symptoms* of relationship failures and not the changes in lifestyles and the mentality of couples. Courts have been involved in financial settlements and child custody battles with ineffective outcomes. However, these legal mechanisms have not addressed the growing relationship needs and couples' expectations in modern societies. Governments have not yet dealt with the changes in people's attitude, which is the cause of all the existing conflicts in relationships. People's mindset, especially at the time of terminating their once precious relationships, is the matter requiring an immediate attention.

862. The main mental adjustments required for couples, as listed in Chapter Twelve (Point 784 above), should guide the public in handling their relationships. People should also push the society and governments to make the needed changes. They must recommend methods and a relationship framework that might bring *objectivity* back into relationships.
863. Furthermore, social mechanisms must be revamped to support the new social mentality and relationship needs.

864. The overall role for governments and people to adjust the required social mechanisms are:
- Support and propagate the idea of partners' individuality and independence.
- Support and propagate the idea of partners' financial responsibility.
- Support and teach the details of the 'relationship framework' to the public.
- Support the idea of time-bounded relationships in legal channels.
- Support and propagate the idea of relationships being viewed as an independent entity like a business enterprise. The concept of R-entity.
- Support and spread the idea of limiting the government role in relationships.
- Support, and participate in, all kinds of research to enhance the quality of a universal 'relationship framework.' GARP and the relationship framework should replace the outmoded guidelines of religion and inefficient laws.

865. The existing asset distribution mechanism at the time of separation is a silly copout. It has evolved only because courts are not equipped to make a fair assessment of relationship issues and financial assets.

866. People and governments are unaware of the ambiguity, confusion, and damages (both financial and emotional) that the existing social mechanisms are causing for relationships and society as a whole.

867. Governments are busy with so many socioeconomic matters already to worry about relationship failures. Therefore, they just deal with the symptoms of this social chaos the best they can at a high cost to taxpayers.

868. If couples did not depend on courts to grant them financial compensation for being in a relationship, their true mentality would manifest before entering their relationships and

many couples would not end up in bad relationships merely based on trust.

869. The absence of government to meddle with relationship decisions would strengthen the concept of individualism. It would empower couples' sense of independence when the responsibility of taking care of their personal interests is left to them.

870. With less government intervention, suddenly partners realize the need to be more proactive and blunt. They would try to find ways to protect themselves in case their relationship fails. They would now really exercise their authority as independent individuals and prepare a *contract* that outlines their expectations. It particularly provides the clear terms of settlement in case of terminating their relationship.

871. The concept of couples signing a contract for their relationship is not new or unromantic. In the older and more practical cultures and religions, for many centuries, a form of contract has helped couples stipulate their expectations and boundaries. It is only in the new cultures where most people consider signing a contract unromantic.

872. Whether couples' decisions at the time of signing a contract would be perfect or not is irrelevant because they, as independent individuals, make those decisions.

873. Of course, couples can always depend on professional advice to prepare the right contract for them. In addition, when new mechanisms are in place, many standard documents will be available for couples to choose a proper relationship model and the type of contract that best suits their needs.

874. The absence of government makes couples smarter and more cautious about their relationships. This new approach would change people's mindset and attitude. There will be less unsuitable relationships. And couples stay in their relationships longer, because they have initially thought through the stages of their relationships more realistically, especially the sad ending that most relationships must face nowadays.

875. The modification of government role in relationships has the highest impact on the financial independence of partners. Instead of letting courts decide about the distribution of assets at the time of separation, partners should agree, independently and objectively, on a system that fits their expectations in their initial marriage contract.
876. The welfare of the public and the prosperity of society are the main objectives of any government. As such, it has a responsibility to support a type of relationship framework that can help partners' needs most effectively and efficiently. Governments cannot leave this important task to chance and hope that things would work out nicely on their own in society.
877. The relationship framework, models, needs, and mechanisms, must be taught in high schools. There should be strict rules for passing these mandatory courses. They are more important than sex education and many other courses.
878. Governments should become a lot more conscientious and active in teaching people how to budget and live within their means. Governments' role to push consumerism to strengthen the economy is coming at the cost of family destructions and imminent social catastrophe.
879. The benefits of having a term (for automatic annulment of marriage) specified in relationship contracts are substantial. Just to mention a few, it will:
    - Change the whole social mentality about relationships.
    - Guarantee partners' needs for individualism and independence.
    - Satisfy the instinctual urges of humans (for companionship and procreation) without unnecessary formalities.
    - Free partners from feeling trapped.
    - Keep partners hopeful about future and happiness if their relationship fails.
    - Make partners smarter about life and their relationship decisions.

- Increase partners' enthusiasm to learn and practice the 'relationship framework' and GARP.
- Introduce a progressive and productive mindset for partners.
- Increase love and cooperation in relationships.
- Enforce teamwork and give it a more crucial role in relationships.
- Increase the longevity of relationships.
- Make children's lives less stressful and more predictable.
- Reduce stress in families and society as a whole.
- Reduce the sense of possessiveness and jealousy.
- Reduce the burden on court systems substantially.
- Eliminate the need for couples to spend outrageous legal fees.
- Reduce the fear of getting into relationships and facing its hassles.
- Increase economic productivity and social welfare due to reduced stress and time wasted on relationship wars between partners.

880. Governments should also abandon their role in regulating, and ruling about, relationships. This would push couples to depend on themselves and teamwork to manage the terms of their contracts.

881. While governments should stay clear of direct interference with relationship conflicts largely, they must support universities and other scholars to develop the relationship framework and GARP.

882. Although many couples use nannies, still the matter of raising children, versus following one's career, has become sensitive these days. One way to settle this issue is to make the partner who insists on having children accept the main role in raising them while the methods and degree of the other partner's involvement are also negotiated in advance and recorded in the marriage contract.

883. The question of having kids at all would become even more crucial in the future. It will become essential to decide carefully whether partners are prepared and capable of raising children.
884. Sometime in the far future, people might even be given a right to sue their parents for bringing them into this world or the way they have raised them. This would be a good policy for making people more responsible for creating children, who might suffer in dysfunctional families, corrupt societies, and polluted environments.
885. Making children should become a calculated decision by intelligent parents rather than a selfish act to enrich their own lives, or even for the socioeconomic purposes of governments.

The Timetable to Make Radical Changes

We have some choices to reverse the deteriorating trends in relationships, yet we must wait for some events and conditions to take their natural courses. During this timeframe, a large number of radical remedies, like the ones suggested in this book are implemented gradually. Although the following timeline for an overhaul of relationships extends over many decades, every single choice and action in that direction would have some immediate benefits for everybody. Even our simple grasp of the points raised in this book and making moderate adjustments in our mentality about relationships would help us directly and toward a more progressive and effective society.

886. Unfortunately, the scope of relationship problems is not still pressing people enough to take serious steps. Therefore, the situation will continue to get worse before people begin to appreciate the need for changing their mentalities and approaches.

887. Meanwhile, couples' expectations keep rising not only from relationships, but also in terms of finding the right partner for themselves. Everybody looks for a partner with higher qualities than themselves and better than their past spouses. This is a mathematically unattainable demand that is emerging in society. The matter gets especially impractical when they seek love in a partner who must also be trustworthy, attractive, and intelligent.
888. In addition to the rising egotistical nature of humans overall, people would continue to have even a harder time to get along with the opposite genders.
889. People are not prepared to be in relationships. Especially, nowadays, they have been brought up to strive for happiness, and to them companionship is only another means of capturing that elusive happiness. They like to ignore that the hardships of life and relationships remain an inevitable reality regardless of their naïve expectations and slogans.
890. Therefore, for the next 40-50 years, gender equality wars and conflicts will escalate and prevent people from finding common grounds for negotiating their needs and lowering their expectations from relationships.
891. The deterioration will be measured by the rising divorce rate (including separations). However, other indicators will confirm the downfall, too, such as people's rising stress in relationships and society as well as the rate of unmarried people in various age categories.
892. A divorce rate of over 75% will probably be reached in 2060s. Then the alarming trends might start an initial social interest to study relationships more seriously and consider some radical solutions more systematically. Governments and scholars will get involved more actively.
893. Various types of research will be needed to define a workable relationship framework and principles. Of course, the progress depends on the global economic condition at that time, as it will deeply affect the state of relationships in the

future. With the high likelihood of a global economic collapse and the demise of consumerism, relationship issues might become of secondary importance when people must struggle for the basic means of survival.

894. On the other hand, economic gloom might inject some sense of reality into relationships. Couples might learn to revert to their traditional mentality and lower their expectations from both life and relationships.

895. However, let us assume that we can succeed to continue with some form of 'a better managed' capitalism and moderate consumerism. We would most likely continue to grapple with new socioeconomic hurdles. These shocks, like the debt crises in the fall of 2008 and the summer of 2011, will haunt us for many years, but then finally make us change our mentality. We might at least learn that deregulation and completely 'free enterprise' leads to chaos.

896. Yet, considering humans' appetite for greed and corruption, we might be heading for big troubles. This means more relationship problems, too, due to stressful economic conditions and uncertainties.

897. Probably by 2080s, with a divorce rate over 80%, the public will acknowledge the need for change. It will be a period of reflection and realizing that the roles and games that couples are playing (e.g., to demand both dependence and independence) are only hurting them. They will understand the need to adjust their expectations from relationships. Then, the relationship framework, and the principles proposed by scholars, might find wide support.

898. Most likely, the need for independence and individuality will still be a dominant factor and thus set the tone for the upcoming relationship guidelines. Nevertheless, we would make sure relationship principles fit the requirements of the society and the emerging progressive norms. A foundation is created to oversee the development and dissemination of relationship principles.

899. Aside from interest and patience, it will take couples a few decades to digest the need for radical changes and adopt a more progressive mindset about relationships. More education is provided to the public, especially at high schools, to propagate the relationship needs and framework.
900. By the end of the 21st century, people might eventually learn the art of being independent financially and emotionally instead of only pretending it. More natural communication, and less role-playing and games, will find common appeal in order to reinstate trust and integrity in relationships.
901. It will take another couple of decades for people to get comfortable with the relationship framework and principles. The new mindset will gradually find full acceptance and couples feel comfortable using the new processes and guidelines. Social mechanisms, including court systems, will be equipped to handle the new setup. This will bring us to the year 2115.
902. It will take 30-40 years for the relationship framework and principles to become a natural setting in society. This will bring us to 2150.
903. Good luck; that is the best the author can hope for. Yet, he would be thrilled to be proven wrong if by some miracle the state of relationships begins to improve much faster than the above depressing dates.

Epilogue

Yes, we should be concerned about the destiny of love and relationships. Neither love nor relationships can serve us the way we expect them to merge and make us happy. In fact, the more we seek love, the more our relationships are becoming unmanageable and shallow. And conversely, the more we need relationships to sooth our loneliness, the less we must rely on love to accomplish our naïve ideals about companionship. Instead, we must try to become practical, learn how to relate effectively, and use realistic criteria for success in our relationships.

The fact is that we have reached an impasse about the meaning of love, because most people remain both hopeful and sceptical about the meaning and application of love for building relationships. We are also weary about the future of relationships if present trends and social mentality prevail. Yet we all have this naïve optimism about love and relationships somehow working according to our imagination and dreams. We hate to face the harsh reality that our perceptions of love and relationships are in no ways in line with the possibilities of the modern society. The question is how much longer we like to deceive ourselves with our idealism and let 'love industry' continue fooling people with all the nonsense about love and whimsical desires. Nonetheless, it seems that we are reaching the point of saturation and the whole masquerade would come to a standstill very soon, when most of us fail to attain even a small chance of having a relatively reliable companion.

Being Good and Enlightened

All the facts, trends, and choices numerated in this book bring us to a simple and obvious conclusion: For building a *manageable* relationship, partners should be *good and enlightened* persons first.

Obviously, becoming a good and enlightened person would be the most natural approach for building a good relationship (and life), if partners could suppress their Ego and become humble humans. Actually, the incentives for becoming better humans are substantial, considering our eagerness to find happiness and an ideal companion. One thing is certain though: Our conventional use of Ego or Model to find and keep our soul mate is definitely doomed. It has failed all along in recent decades. It has brought us only more loneliness and frustrations and it would never get us the spiritual love that we seek. However, becoming a good and enlightened person is a difficult task too.

Being a 'good' person mostly refers to a well-balanced personality, with an emphasis on Self, and the least amount of Ego. This person has a higher chance of building a practical relationship, because he/she has more control over his/her attitude and expectations, and also because he/she believes in the value of a good relationship that is driven by unselfish standards. Model dominance mainly involves phoniness and game playing, which hinder a person's chance for goodness and naturalness. Yet, Model dominance is somewhat less destructive than Ego domination for building relationships. As noted before, both Model and Ego have some positive attributes as well, which, in moderate dosage, might help in building a good relationship. Especially Model can be quite useful in exchanging complimentary gestures and empowering partners' positive interactions when it is done properly.

Assuming that we can learn to become a bit less selfish, the next step is to become as natural as possible by getting rid of all those layers of phoniness, pretensions, neediness, and games. We must really believe that arrogance and playing games would only create more obstacles for building healthy relationships and finding happiness. However, becoming natural is a tough task even if we knew how to do it. For one thing, we cannot overcome our habits and conditional forces in our subconscious. Our modern societies advocate only more superficiality, greed, and games. To some extent, even marriage counsellors are making couples more unnatural when they encourage them to play phony roles. To become natural, we must understand who we are, which starts by assessing our needs and the authenticity of the motives behind them. We must value our independence and integrity more than anything else. We must find our purpose in life instead of only imitating others and accepting social values blindly. While respecting others and their choices, we must curb our desire for their approval of who we are. Most people would have difficulty accepting a simple and needless individual in their close circles, and we should learn to cope with that obstacle without any grudges.

For building successful relationships, partners must be *enlightened* too. 'Enlightened' mainly means that partners are aware of humans' inherent limitations. Accordingly, they have higher sympathy toward each other and also keep their expectations from relationships low. They realize their own flaws and appreciate that their partners often behave according to some inner and outer forces beyond their control too; so their behaviour should not be considered utter malice all the time. A major implication of being *enlightened* is that partners are wise and patient. They know how to apply their goodness effectively in their relationships despite the inevitable disappointments and even occasional hostility between partners.

Only a small group of people has genetic superiority, grows up in enriching environments, or automatically turns into good-natured and enlightened humans. For the rest of us, with mediocre genes and meagre rearing conditions, becoming a good, enlightened person requires major motivation and effort. We must first learn to overcome so many of our idiosyncrasies and personality flaws through self-awareness. It takes special courage, talent, and conviction to acknowledge one's deficiencies and pursue a path of self-awareness. The learning process is long and painful, as it requires new convictions that contradict our phony values and lifestyle. Through awareness, we must learn about ourselves, the interworking of our personality aspects, relationship standards and objectives, and authentic life values. We must be able to forego some of our habits, greed, and jealousy.

The concept of being *good* and *enlightened* is a noble and popular principle in our minds. We know intuitively that, for building an ideal relationship, partners should be good and enlightened individuals who know themselves as well as their relationship needs. However, the problem is that intuitively we always blame others and justify ourselves. We are not objective. Our logic is not strong enough to realize that relationship conflicts cannot always be the fault of our partners. Our crooked logic and Ego have convinced us of our flawlessness. Some of us actually believe to be saints. Some believe to know it all. Therefore, we react negatively toward other individuals' viewpoints and logic relentlessly. We strongly believe that our relationship problems are due to the badness and stupidity of our partners. Therefore, the depth of relationship problems clearly lies in our hasty judgments about, and our misperception of, our partners, instead of realizing our own imperfections. In order to see even the scope of the problems, we must sincerely try to scrap our Ego tendencies and focus on self-awareness rather than making hasty judgment and blaming our partners. This is almost as hard as asking a swimmer to unlearn swimming.

Nonetheless, seldom both partners can be good and Self dominated, which means most of us must find a way to relate by maintaining a good balance of all the three aspects of personality—with Ego contained as much as possible. Ego's force and motives should be somehow controlled through constant improvements in Self and Model, but more importantly, we need a relationship framework to help partners maintain an effective balance among the personality aspects of partners.

For becoming a good person, good genes and rearing background are important. Other than these important factors, self-analysis and leaning about our flaws and needs are the most important means of becoming a good person. The discussions in Appendix 12-A also provide more insights for managing our personality aspects and a method for raising self-awareness.

The Conclusion

It seemed like a good idea to the author to provide a summary of the highlights of discussions in this book. The job proved rather impossible, however, because almost all the points listed in various chapters are important issues that couples need to know and observe for building good relationships. Actually, around 900 points (facts, trends, and choices) in this book have been selected from amongst thousands of related topics about relationships. Therefore, at the end, the best summary would be the points raised in the Introduction, and topics discussed in the three chapters in Part II, as they seem to have some type of urgency for scrutiny. Those trends provide a foundation for building all the other steps necessary for developing a healthy relationship environment urgently. Reading the whole book again, maybe a few times, could actually be a good strategy to strengthen our convictions and change our mindset about relationships. At last, we might agree with the main fact, trend, and choice offered at the beginning of the book. That is, we should eventually admit that:

The Main Fact
Our understanding of love and relationships
is wrong.

The Main Trend
Relationship conflicts have gotten out of hand
and the situation will continue to worsen.

The Main Choice
Only a drastic change in our mentality can save the
future of relationship.

www.ingramcontent.com/pod-product-compliance
Lightning Source LLC
Chambersburg PA
CBHW061759110426
42742CB00012BB/2084